With Intention to Build:
The Unrealized Concepts, Ideas, and Dreams of Moshe Safdie

images
Publishing

Published in Australia in 2020 by
The Images Publishing Group Pty Ltd
ABN 89 059 734 431

Offices
Melbourne
6 Bastow Place
Mulgrave, Victoria 3170
Australia
Tel: +61 3 9561 5544

New York
6 West 18th Street 4B
New York City, NY 10011
United States
Tel: +1 212 645 1111

Shanghai
6F, Building C, 838 Guangji Road
Hongkou District, Shanghai 200434
China
Tel: +86 021 31260822

books@imagespublishing.com
www.imagespublishing.com

NATIONAL LIBRARY OF AUSTRALIA

A catalogue record for this book is available from the National Library of Australia

Title: With Intention to Build: The Unrealized Concepts, Ideas, and Dreams of Moshe Safdie // Safdie Architects (text by Michael J. Crosbie)
ISBN: 9781864708493

Edited by Michael Crosbie and Christopher Mulvey
Book design by Michael Gericke and Matt McInerney

This title was commissioned in IMAGES' Melbourne office and produced as follows:
Editorial Georgia (Gina) Tsarouhas,
Production Nicole Boehringer and Ryan Marshall

MIX
Paper from responsible sources
FSC® C019910
FSC www.fsc.org

Printed and bound in China by Artron Art Group on 160gsm Da Dong FSC® Wood Free paper

Cover image
Sketch, pastel,
Sketchbook 66, Black Friday Munich
Moshe Safdie, 1990

Thesis sketch, Moshe Safdie, 1961

Preface

As an architect committed to building and impacting the environment, I've always considered designs developed without intention of building to be incomplete statements. So much of reality, be it economics, the force of gravity, or construction feasibility can be ignored as to make such architectural productions less relevant. But there is another category of unrealized designs. These are designs conceived with intention to build, resolving the varied forces that constrain and shape architecture, that then, because of external circumstances of one kind or another, remain on the drawing boards. These projects, numerous for every practicing architect, form a fascinating track through a thought process and a career. In the case of my own practice, some of the most significant works have been designed, detailed, and yet not built; significant in the sense that they embody ideas and concepts of great import.

Habitat '67 was realized at the Montreal Expo, but at one fifth of the original concept that we had proposed to the government. The original concept incorporating ideas of mixed-use, integrating community space, and residences would have gone well beyond the realized project in pointing the way to the potential of three-dimensional organization of high-rise building. Had it been built, perhaps the course of architecture over the century would have been different. Similarly, designs for such diverse projects as the Columbus Center in New York, the National Art Museum of China in Beijing, and the National Library of Israel, each in its own way, I believe, would have presented seminal propositions. We have selected some of the more relevant unbuilt projects that have evolved over the course of a 55-year practice, believing that they complement and amplify the architectural intentions presented by our realized projects.

—Moshe Safdie

Moshe Safdie in conversation
with Michael J. Crosbie

The Nature of Unbuilt Architecture

Sketch, ink and pastel,
Sketchbook 37, Columbus Center
Moshe Safdie, 1985

Michael J. Crosbie: In his book, *The Built, the Unbuilt, and the Unbuildable: In Pursuit of Architectural Meaning*, Robert Harbison compares artistic pursuits such as literature, music, painting, and architecture and concludes that the last is exceptionally vulnerable to forces outside the creative process. He notes that we can partake of "unbuilt or half-built" books, paintings, and musical works if their creators lacked the time or will to complete them, but architectural works can't be enjoyed in the same way. What's your view on this vulnerability in architecture?

Etching, *The Well*, Giovanni Battista Piranesi, 1761
Le Carceri d'Invenzione (2nd Edition, Plate 13)

Moshe Safdie: The first act in creating architecture is generally its representation. Is there value in the drawings or the models as representations of ideas? The representation is not the same as a building constructed full scale. Nor does it have to stand the test of gravity or the weather for survival. However, through the history of architecture representations have had lasting power as ideas. Piranesi, for example, didn't represent buildable environments, but certainly his drawings have had an effect on architects for centuries. A more recent example was Antonio Sant'Elia, one of the Italian Rationalists, who never built much. But his drawings still have the power to excite the imagination.

I wouldn't dismiss the representation of unbuilt architecture as valueless, but it's important to differentiate it from real architecture. In our media age that distinction is blurred. Most people's impressions and opinions of architecture come from photographs, itself a representation. How many people form opinions of architecture from having been in it? A shockingly small number. There is a hierarchy and difference between a project that was conceived and sketched out very conceptually, and one that has had the investment of energy, engineering, and detailing that a building receives when there is an intention to construct it. In our collection of unrealized projects, at one end of the spectrum we have the Pompidou Centre—ideas represented in models and drawings. They did not go through intense engineering. At the other end there is the Ballet Opera House and Columbus Center, which was in design development and detailing, working drawings, shop drawings—fully buildable. It can be enjoyed more than just conceptually—as a crafted building. It's important to distinguish between these two types: worked out, fully engineered designs and conceptual projects.

Does architecture have a vulnerability that other arts have, such as an unfinished novel or symphony?

It depends on the art form. In music, if you have the score, you have the work. But you need the performance to enjoy it. Maybe a musician who has perfect pitch can read and hear the music, but most people need the performance. You might argue the same for architecture—if you have

Watercolor and ink painting
Industrial Building with Corner Tower, Antonio Sant'Elia, 1913

the drawings, you could build the building. With a work of literature or painting, once written or painted, it's complete. Architecture is unique in that respect. Its transformation from representation to reality requires lots of energy and resources, unlike most other art forms.

I question the attitudinal difference of some architects embarking on conceptual design. Sometimes I am amazed by an architect's representation that chooses to ignore fundamental physical forces that govern realization. For example, a project that just "floats" out there. As an architect you know it doesn't address structural needs. There might be a 60-foot glass wall represented with little lines of glass division. But to build a wall of that scale you need a frame structure, which is not there. That would change the character of the architecture. When we do competitions, for better or worse (and sometimes I think it's to our disadvantage), we don't draw what we don't think we can build. We are already infusing the design with engineering and detailing.

An unbuilt work of architecture is never "diluted," never value-engineered. It preserves a certain vigor by virtue of its incompletion. Might we think about "unbuilt" as a phase in the life of all projects, completed or not? Aren't there elements in all projects that end up "unbuilt" because of lack of resources or other contingencies?

There's a key word in that question that's worth challenging: diluted. When you conceive of a work that does not test economics, the fabrication capabilities of materials, or gravity and its structural implications, that concept is "freer." But is it less diluted, more sublime? Or just deceptive? To me, meeting the constraints of reality enriches architecture. And if it doesn't enrich architecture, it's conceptually flawed. Say you are interested in transparency, and in your representation you achieve transparency with graphic deception. If in reality a heavy frame must support it, you haven't solved the problem. You haven't created transparency. An architect who really wants to solve it might wrack his brains to come up with a system of cables to support the glass with counterweights. The architect's imagination, technology, engineering, and material capability come together to create something that's very exciting—you know it's real. The more architects are inclined not to deceive they will solve the problem they intend to. For example, for Habitat II New York we were looking at 40 to 50 floors of load-bearing structure—heavy and inefficient. Could we use a frame to insert the units into? I rejected that idea because the material technology did not encourage that direction. But a suspension structure—cables in tension—could be a lightweight way to support them. The elements could be lightweight, repetitive modules attached to cables, held by a superstructure of masts and pillars. We wanted a sense of repetitiveness and lightness in a modular system. Conceptually it was on the road to being buildable.

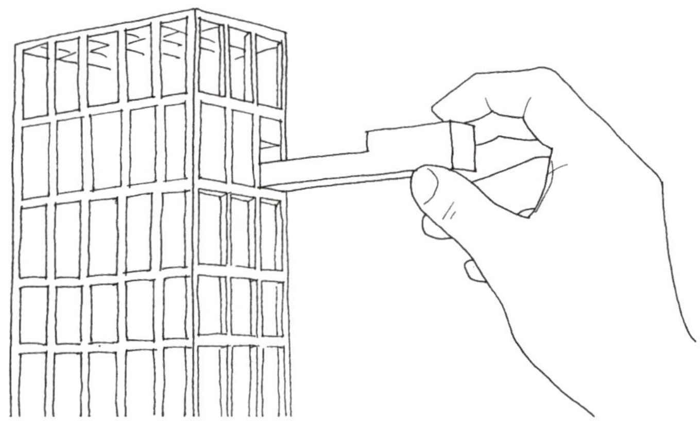

Maison Loucheur (unbuilt), Le Corbusier, 1929

How do unbuilt projects inform the way you interact with clients and move projects forward? How does unbuilt work enhance your work on future projects?

I've never thought about that question. Going back to my Habitat days, there was some accumulated impact of the succession of unbuilt projects: Puerto Rico, New York, Washington. My own reaction (which sometimes I regret) was to retreat, in a desperation to build. I felt this deep need to build, and out of that came projects like Cold Spring in Baltimore—basically traditional construction. They were not as big a departure from convention as Habitat was. But there was a great sense of wanting to build something. Not having that opportunity led to depression, it was discouraging. But then you get out of it. It teaches you about how many disappointments can you sustain, and the impact of that on your work as an architect.

This idea of making a breakthrough—in your case, did that extend to your interaction with future potential clients and programs?

For me it was an inverse experience. I designed this impossible building that somehow gets built. Then you spend the next ten years of your life trying to do more in that realm of experimentation. And it doesn't work: Habitat 1, 2, 3, 4, 5, Pompidou Centre, San Francisco State College. The escape was to do mediocre work for developers. But in Israel came a different kind of escape: projects that dealt with history and context, not about technology. Geography was the escape.

A critique of some authors is that they write the same book over and over again. This is also the case with some architects: One thinks of Mies designing the same building repeatedly. Do you think such re-occurrence exists in your own oeuvre, and if so what roles do unbuilt projects play in this?

That's a big question. It is the issue between a dominant, singular language of an architect versus the variables in which he functions. Maybe that's the most profound question of contemporary architecture. Centuries ago architects functioned within a certain cultural and technological context—the framework in which they operated. Then we come to a whole world of new possibilities with materials with the International Style. There is a tendency to start developing a vocabulary and applying it to different building types, locations, sites, and you see the struggle. Le Corbusier does his white buildings, but when he gets to India he can't go on doing that. Something about India makes him do something different, like the Villa Sarabhai or the Mill Owners' Association Building. He starts using concrete and brick in different ways. In our own time most architects have chosen to develop a powerful vocabulary that dominates most of what they do, regardless of building type, location, and program.

In my case there are themes that carry over from project to project, even in the unbuilt work. For example, a roof geometry developed for Wichita becomes an important element in India, in the Khalsa Heritage Centre.

Buckminster Fuller Dome, 1961

Transparent, shell-like roofs that evolve at the United States Institute of Peace find expression in another project in Brazil, but become like sitting under a leafy tree. It changes because of the location. We might use precast in Montreal or Washington, but then you design for a place that does not do much precast construction, and you explore other masonry. The language is very different, and this might have put me in trouble with certain critics who have felt there is an uneven consistency in what I do. But there are a lot of themes or ideas that, consciously or subconsciously, are explored and transformed from project to project. It's evolutionary, because evolution is about mutations that stick. In architecture, ideas evolve though a mutative process—when they have validity, they stick. You have to have a critical capacity to say it's worth keeping that mutation or not.

Is the consistency in your approach the desire to open yourself to these mutations, to evolve?

It's a combination of curiosity and fear of boredom. It's true that when I go for interviews, particularly with developers, there is this unease—what are they going to get? Unless you have very courageous clients like Alice Walton, who didn't know what we would do at Crystal Bridges [Museum of American Art], but she loved the Skirball Cultural Center and knew she wasn't going to get that. Developer clients have this desire about you showing them something. But it's like roulette for them.

You've written that "Architecture is a tectonic, material medium; inherent buildability must be deeply imbedded in the process." Can you talk about inherent buildabilty in your unbuilt projects? How does it inform the design process from the first stroke?

If an architect doesn't have a profound understanding of the capabilities and behavior of materials and structural systems, he can't be a good architect. It doesn't matter how great the team of engineers working with him are. Without understanding the organic nature of these things, conceptually, it can't be informed by the engineering forces in the building, for example. An architect must have enough understanding of the nature of materials and structure to conceive the nature of the structure. Buckminster Fuller made me realize that we have a moral obligation to build with minimal resources because that is the way to maximize what humankind can produce in terms of shelter and cities. When you see a use of materials that feels right, you can achieve great architecture. When you conceive of architecture in ways that are not efficient, your concept is flawed. I think this idea of inherent buildability should drive the curriculum of architecture schools.

Inherent buildability is a presence sitting with you all the time when you are designing?

Yes, and it's not like I've got it all up my sleeve. We started a project three weeks ago and today we met with the engineers. We have a few ideas about how this 20-story building could be structured and framed. We got positive support to go in one direction over another. That's what happens in competitions—we might have just three weeks to consider structural and environmental systems. I hate it when a client says, "Just make me a rendering." You can't. It's very superficial.

[Louis] Kahn worked very much in this way.

He was very much like that, and he romanticized it, which actually was quite inspiring—his conversation with a brick. You can have that kind of conversation with a brick, with wood, with every element in your building. [Frank Lloyd] Wright spoke about it differently, but was also very much like this. When he would find a methodology, like his concrete-block houses, it would generate his whole conceptual approach.

In reflecting on your time working with Kahn in Philadelphia, how do you see your own relationship with colleagues and collaborators in your firm?

I was with Kahn as an apprentice, which is very much how he structured his practice. I attained a degree of responsibility in the year I was there, but not the same as that of his trusted lieutenants, like Carles Vallhonrat or David Kurdish. Each was in his own right a gifted architect. Kahn was not, once you departed his sphere, very generous. I think I've changed a lot over the past 20 years. I was of the mindset that I could do it all alone, that I just needed support. But now I have built a team, a second

Model, City Tower, Philadelphia PA
Louis I. Kahn and Anne G. Tyng (associated architects), 1956–1957

generation in the office. They are in their 30s and 40s, and most of them have been here since they graduated, mentored by those with more experience. It's amazing to see such an extremely talented team who have internalized firm values regarding the importance of constructability, materiality, respect for the program and climate, what makes a building work—totally shared. They have grown as professionals in this environment and culture. Our practice hovers around 80 people, with great efficiency and output. I don't think Kahn ever had that. Many young people would come and go. There was a shortage of people who grew with that practice. But here we discover things together; the relationships are not transactional. It's a very supportive and collegial environment. It's like a family, in that sense.

What did you learn in your work with Kahn that you brought to your own practice?

I learned how to be an architect from beginning to end. From the day you meet a client and see the site, to the day the building is occupied. Momentum is significant in the making of architecture. Often the relationships extend beyond the project, into subsequent projects with our clients.

The Unbuilt Projects

Sketch, pastels
Sketchbook 66, Black Friday Munich
Moshe Safdie, 1990

Habitat Original Proposal

Montreal, Canada
1964

The original Habitat proposal was conceived as a sector of the city with residential, commercial, and institutional facilities integrated within a single complex. Inclined surfaces, like grand hillsides, form the complex's residential component, oriented toward unobstructed views and sunlight. Partially sheltered on grade are parking and transportation facilities, shops, schools, office space, and an extensive network of parks connecting with the city.

The original proposal consists of one 12-story section and one 22-story section, with a total of 1200 housing units, a 350-room hotel, two schools, and a neighborhood shopping area. The design was presented to the Cabinet of Canada for approval as the primary theme exhibit of the 1967 World Exposition in Montreal. The government decided to build only a small part of the proposal—158 housing units within a 12-story section—which was subsequently redesigned as Habitat '67.

Sketch, Moshe Safdie, 1963

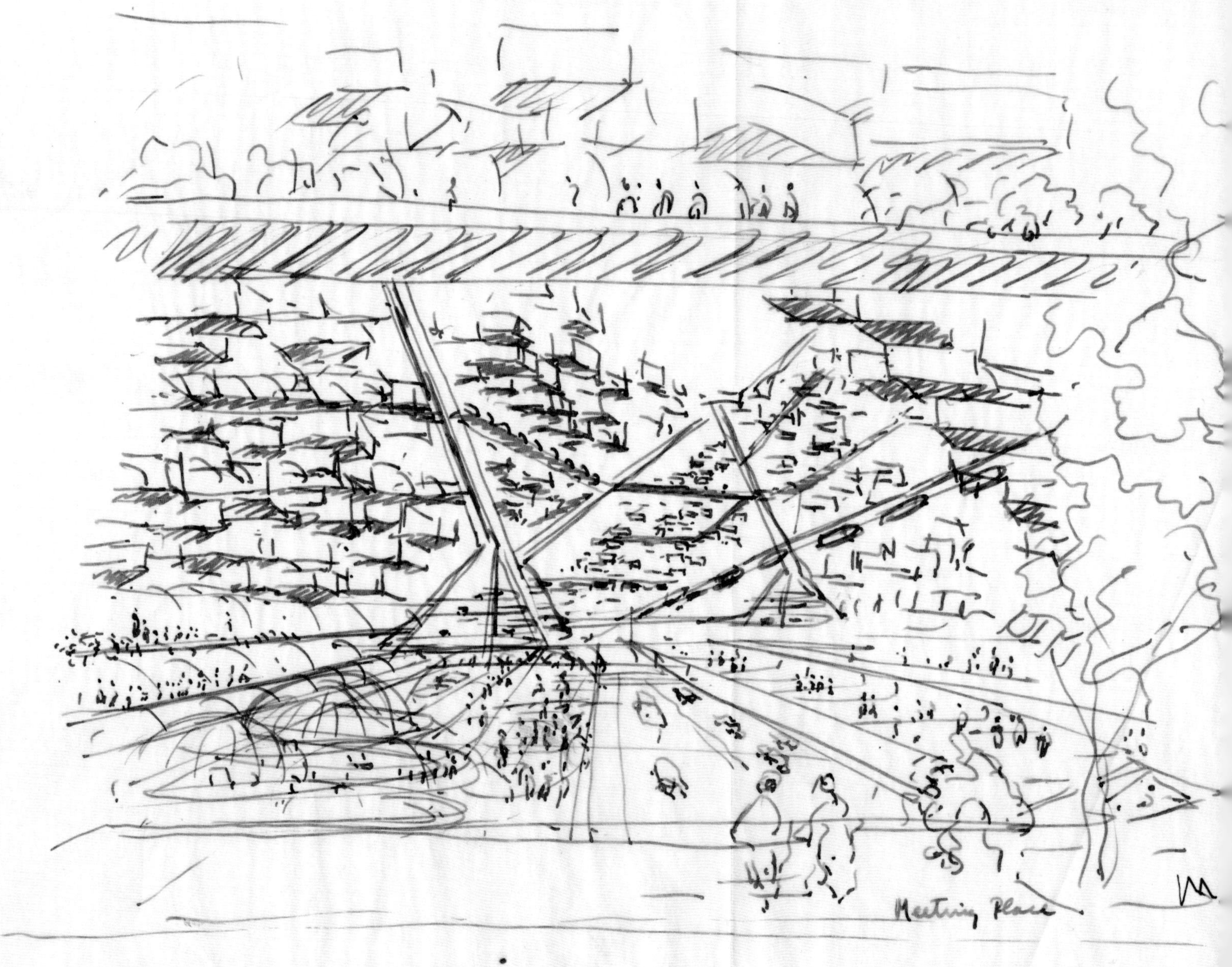

HABITAT 167

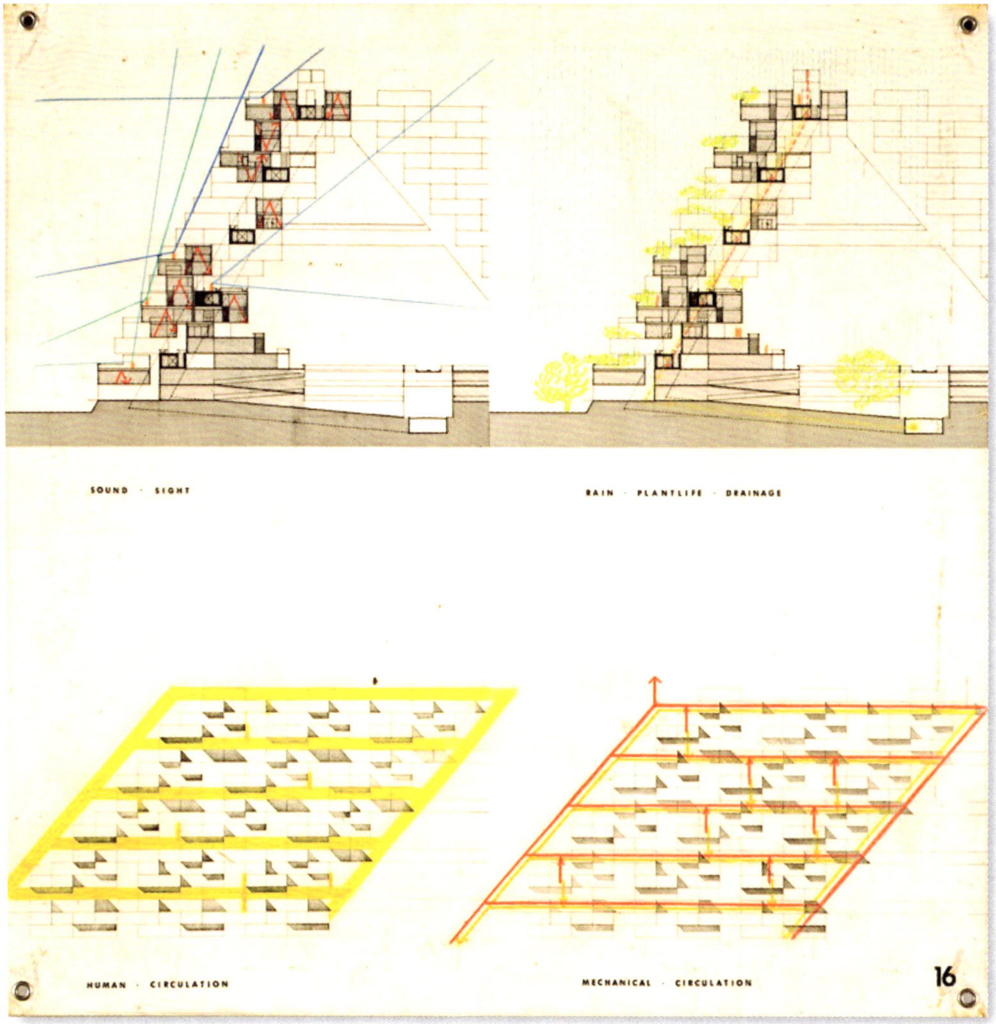

Presentation drawing
Moshe Safdie, 1964

Left: Sketch, ink on trace paper
Moshe Safdie, 1963

The original Habitat design seems much more oriented toward city making, creating an urban place. What did it teach you about urban place making?

It was a genesis of thinking about different uses stacked three dimensionally, with street systems occurring at different levels. You can start optimizing different uses within the matrix. This is an idea that re-occurs in our work. You would think Chongqing, China, would be an ideal project to go in that direction—and some of the early sketches explore that. But in that context it was impossible to realize some of these ideas. When people ask, "What is the one project you hope to do that you haven't?" it is the three-dimensional city of that complexity and scale, which was suggested in Habitat. You need enough scale, density, ownership, and administrative municipal maintenance that can deal with all the multilevel public right-of-way. It was surprisingly sophisticatedly worked out.

Model, Axial and plan view
(132 x 41 x 11 inches H), 1964

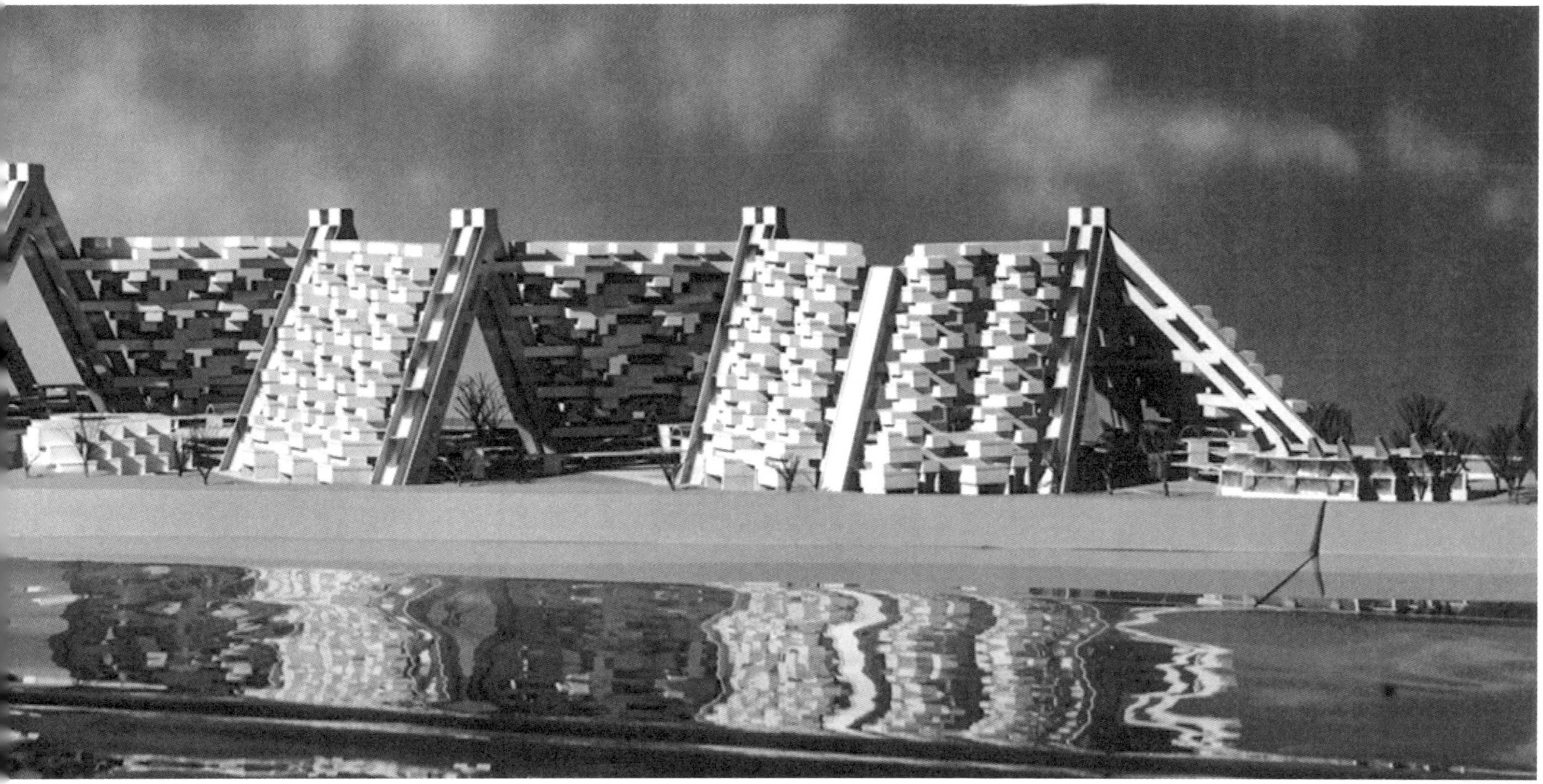

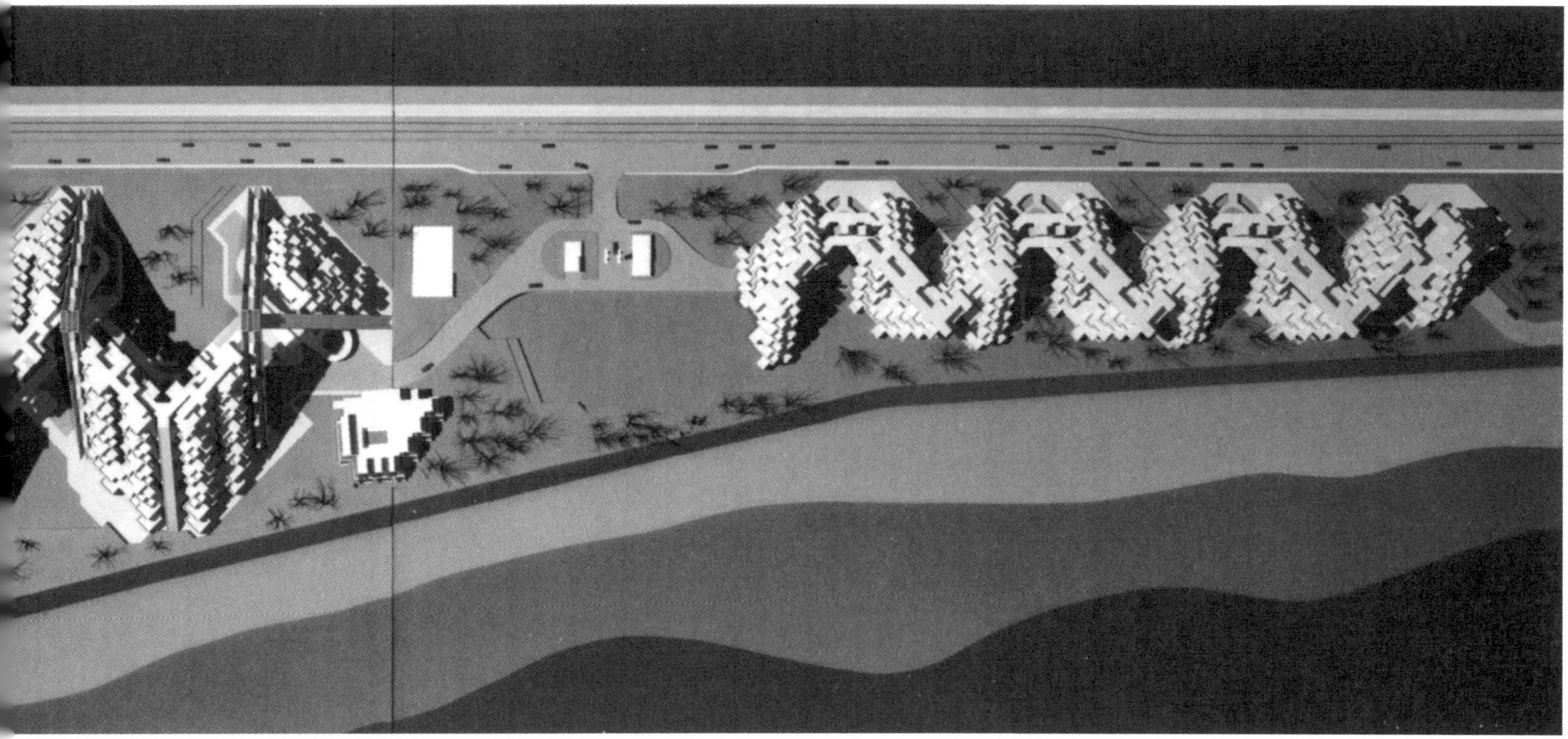

It started with a little diagram of office and residential towers, and I began rearranging them. There was the idea of taking the mixed use of a residential city, with an FAR [floor area ratio] of 12+, and making it more livable, efficient, light sensitive, secure, with multiple circulation options. It was an interpretation of an idea that was out there—thinking about the city three dimensionally. It resulted in some interesting plans. One standard we set was that the residential units should face the sun, either southeast, southwest, or south. So we ended up with the rhomboids stacking, all of the planes facing the sun. That was an amazing invention: you could stack the planes facing the sun and they would support each other.

Model (132 x 41 x 11 inches H), 1964

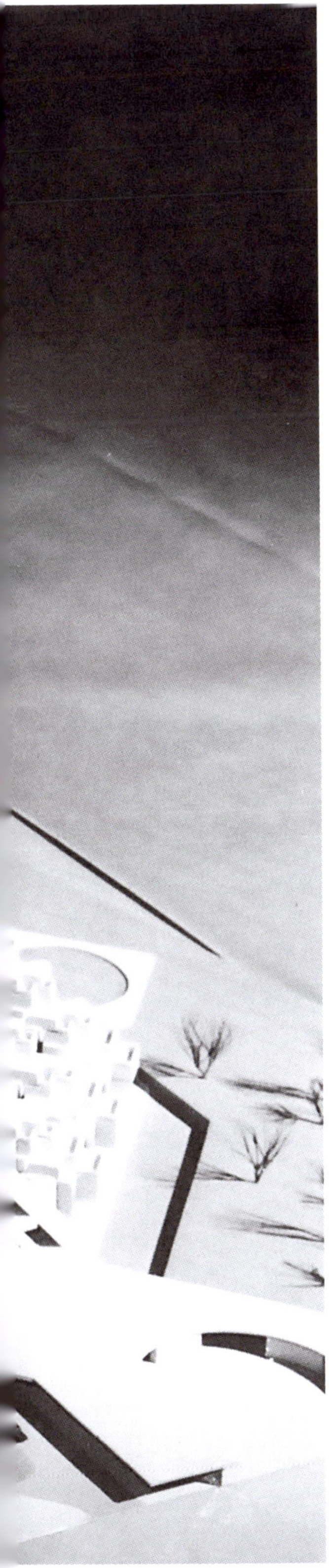

Left: Model (132 x 41 x 11 inches H), 1964

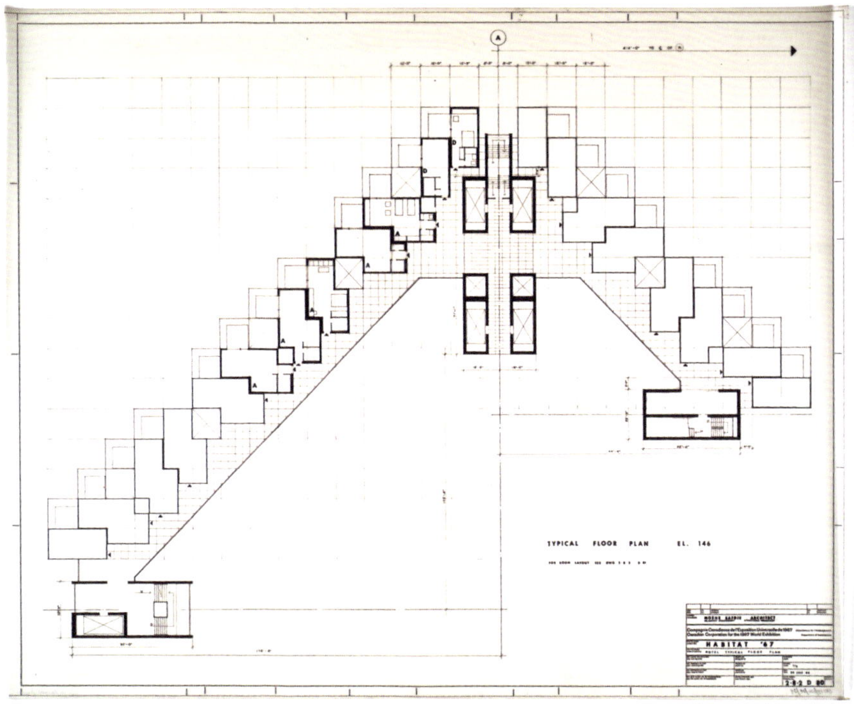

Construction drawings
Floor plan and section of hotel component, 1964

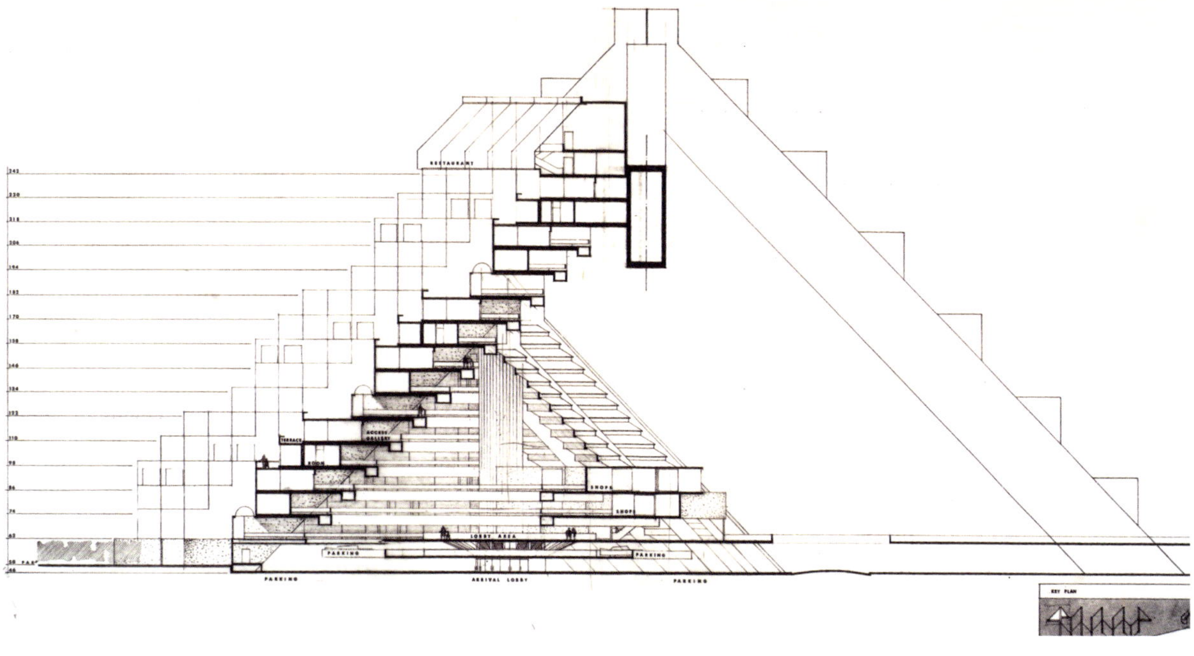

San Francisco State College Student Union

San Francisco, California, USA
1967–1968

This design contains offices and study areas, student stores, dining halls, classrooms, and meeting rooms for the college's 20,000 students. Located at the hub of campus pedestrian movement, the U-shaped scheme channels circulation through the building and creates a meeting place integral to the busy central campus green. A continuous network of stairs, landings, and entrances distinguishes the building's exterior. With interior stairs and elevators, the extensive circulation allows students to access the union day and night. The structure's interlocking system of various-sized hexagonal modules make up glazed and landscaped sloping façades. These connect through a system of hinging and pivoting walls, permitting flexibility for interior spaces. The precast concrete modules could be mass-produced and easily assembled on site.

Initiated and approved by the students, the design was rejected in 1968 by the College Board of Trustees, inciting campus riots.

Rendering, colored pencil, Carlos Diniz, 1967

Model, view from west, 1967

You've observed that politics is often not a friend of architecture. Of all your unbuilt projects, that seems most true of the San Francisco State College Student Union. How did that political dynamic manifest itself and end the project?

Actually, I would correct what I said: Politics is a fundamental ingredient. When it's on your side, you can do everything. Look at what Wallace Harrison achieved with the support of the Rockefellers in Albany: When you've got the king on your side—when I had Teddy Kollek on my side in Jerusalem, or Kevin White in Boston—it's amazing. When it's not on your side, you're screwed. San Francisco State was a minor campus building, but it became a cause célèbre because of the moment in time, the cultural impact of the students' revolt, and the state administration. Reagan was governor and Charles Luckman was on the state's Board of Trustees. They saw a campus of rabble-rousers and hippies. It was like the clash of two worlds. The impact of the rejection of the design was profound. There were riots and the college brought in a new president. Wild times.

Digital rendering, 2019

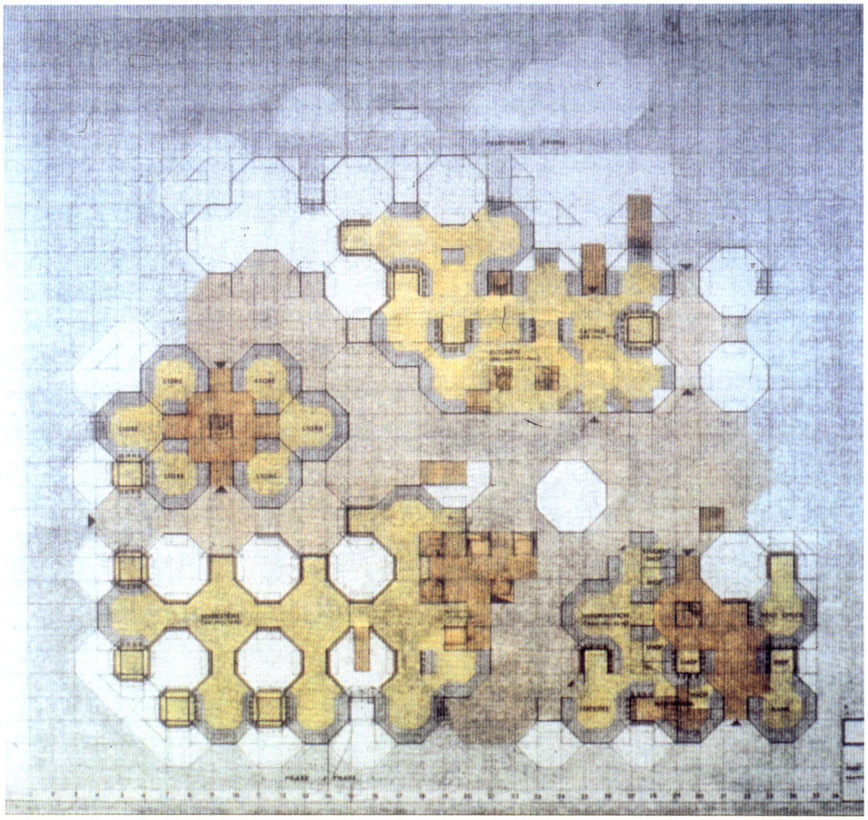

I think the building is pretty radical. I sometimes wonder if it had been built, what would it look like today, because it had a lot of issues—underside spaces where the stairs go up on the façade, waterproofing slopes that have grass on them. It was a building with craft issues, but I feel we would have probably solved them.

Floor plan drawing, ink and color tone on vellum, 1968

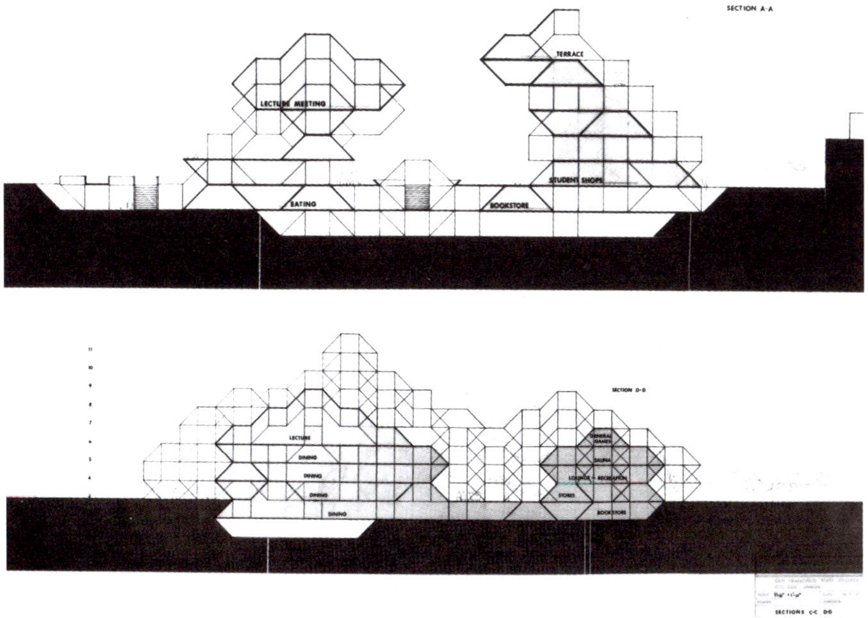

Diagrammatic section drawings, 1967

Left: Model (29 x 24 x 15 inches H), 1967

Opposite: Model, interior view, 1967

The Daily Gater

Volume 98, Number 34 | San Francisco State College | Thursday, March 28, 1968

Trustees postpone College Union vote

The College Union design went back to committee after an inconclusive discussion by the Board of Trustees yesterday.

Many Trustees liked architect Moshe Safdie's unique, complex plans, but some of them thought that they are incompatible with the rest of the campus, according to Margaret Nixon, executive secretary of the College Union Council (CUC).

"They put off a decision for not more than 60 days. Their campus building and grounds committee will come to SF State to study the campus before they take it up again," Mrs. Nixon said after she and Safdie presented the model of the Union to the Trustees.

The cubist, idiomatic scheme of the College Union must be approved by the board before construction can begin. If all goes smoothly, ground may be broken this summer on the current site of the huts.

Safdie, the young Montreal architect who developed the "modular unit" concept of design, will be on campus after Spring vacation to present the model and plans of the College Union to the students.

Albert Duro, a student member of the CUC, said that students' responses to the Union plans may have a large effect on the Trustees decision.

"Both in terms of architecture and in terms of function, it will probably be the best student union building ever built. I expect that the students and the Trustees will recognize that," Duro said.

Pictures of the union were released in yesterday's Gater and Open Process. Tomorrow's Gater will include a report of the uses of the building.

The Trustees' finance committee will investigate the Union's financing in the interim. Duro, who is also the CUC's finance committee chairman, said that he sees no problem there.

Architect Safdie stands behind proposed Union model

Colossal petition drive

Art students support Union

A colossal petition drive to blitz the Board of Trustees into accepting Moshe Safdie's unique College Union concept will begin today, boosted by an outraged band of art students.

The artists—infuriated by a Trustees committee rejection of the Union for its "incompatibility" with SF State's other buildings — sculpted a model that the Trustees would accept.

"It's built of square blocks and topped by a capitalist symbol that the Trustees should love—a Nazi footlocker," one of the designers said with a sneer.

The new Union proposal is located in the Art Department sculpture yard.

"It's great. I'm constantly surprised by how much support Moshe's design has here," said AS Vice President Albert Duro, the spearhead of the petition push.

Art students designed a "compatible" College Union for the Trustees

Duro and the other hard core Union backers will set up a table in front of the Commons between 10 a.m. and 2 p.m. everyday until the Trustees gather again Wednesday of next week. They will collect signatures and conduct other "agitation and propaganda work" in this location, Duro said.

Instructors will also circulate the petition in their classes, he added.

The 11 story high Union would be located on the present site of the Commons and huts. If the Trustees okay the project next week, ground will be broken "around May Day," Duro said. The key first phase will be finished about 1½ years after it is started.

Construction of the first phase will require destruction of the huts and the Coffee Shops entire seating area, at minimum. The AS and the SF State Foundation are still trying to figure out what to do when this occurs.

A recent recommendation by Safdie's San Francisco associates and the chancellor's staff architects would move the Union 30 feet north, taking out most of the Redwood Room for the first phase.

"The Trustees felt that the Union would be visibly too close to the Library unless it was moved. But remember, the Union would slope away from the Library," said Franklin Sheehan, the Administration's man in charge of the College Union.

The 30-foot move is only a recommendation, not a final decision, Sheehan emphasized.

Front pages of *The Daily Gater*, daily newspaper at San Francisco State College. Top: March 28, 1968; Bottom: October 14, 1968

Cover of *Revolution*, twice-monthly publication at San Francisco State College; March 15, 1969

Habitat II New York

New York, New York, USA
1967–1968

During design, the project site moved several miles down the East River to a district of unused piers south of Brooklyn Bridge. The new site presented the challenge of developing a tower-scale Habitat. A density requirement of 300 per acre surpasses previous Habitats, along with a city requirement that the building maintain access and views to the river. Rethinking the structural logic of the project, ultralight units are suspended from catenary cables like a suspension bridge. The concrete-encased cables anchor at the top to three towers containing elevator cores and mechanical services, and at the bottom to a compression beam and multilevel structure holding a million square feet of office and commercial space. Together, the towers, cables, and compression beam are akin to the mast and boom of a sailboat.

The project did not go forward due to faltering developer interest in realizing it.

Model, 1968

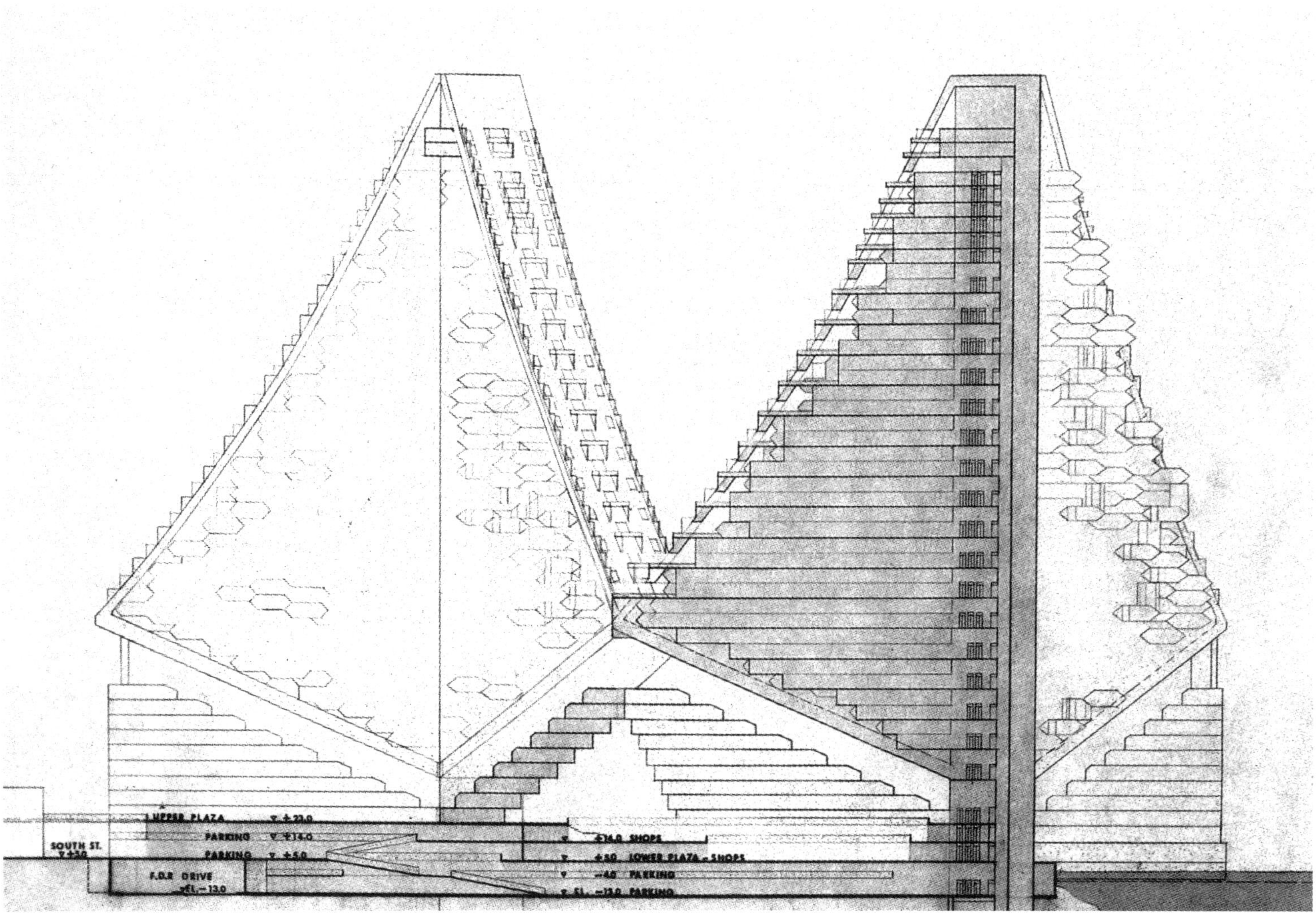

Cross-section drawing, 1968

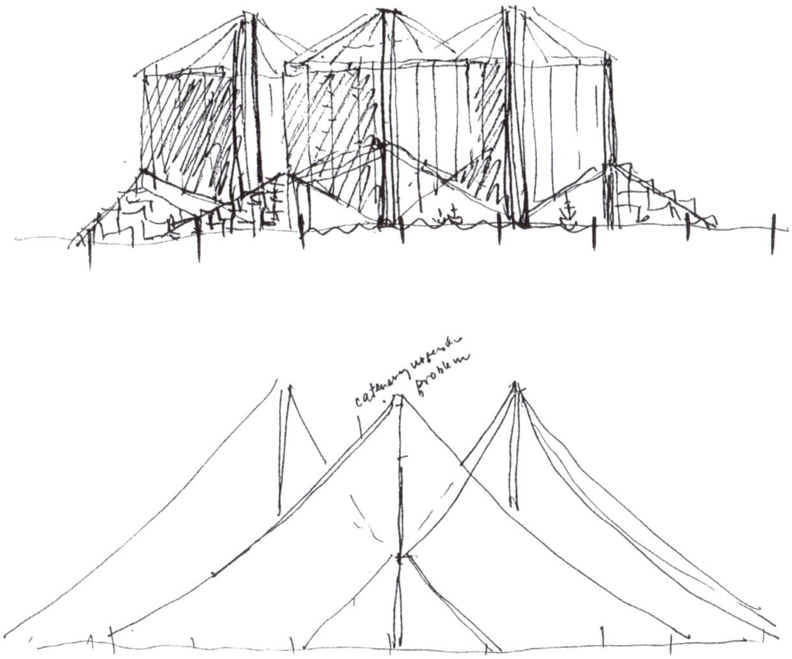

Sketches. Catenary structural systems. Moshe Safdie, 1968

Model, 1968

How was Habitat II in New York informed by Habitat in Montreal? What did it teach you about the possibilities of departing from that design to meet the context of New York—also the inherent buildability of each of these projects?

We learned from Habitat that standardization was difficult because of the load-bearing elements. Going up three times as high made it impossible to be load bearing. Habitat II was over the water. If the foundation system could be concentrated instead of spread out, it would work better.

What do you do? In the first New York Habitat we tried a space frame. But it was clear that the frame would not have standard members because those at the top would be smaller than those at the bottom. Conceptually, the idea of hanging it could be the answer. You concentrate the structure in big-scale elements of masts and cores, and hang it all. You could span with trusses and hang it.

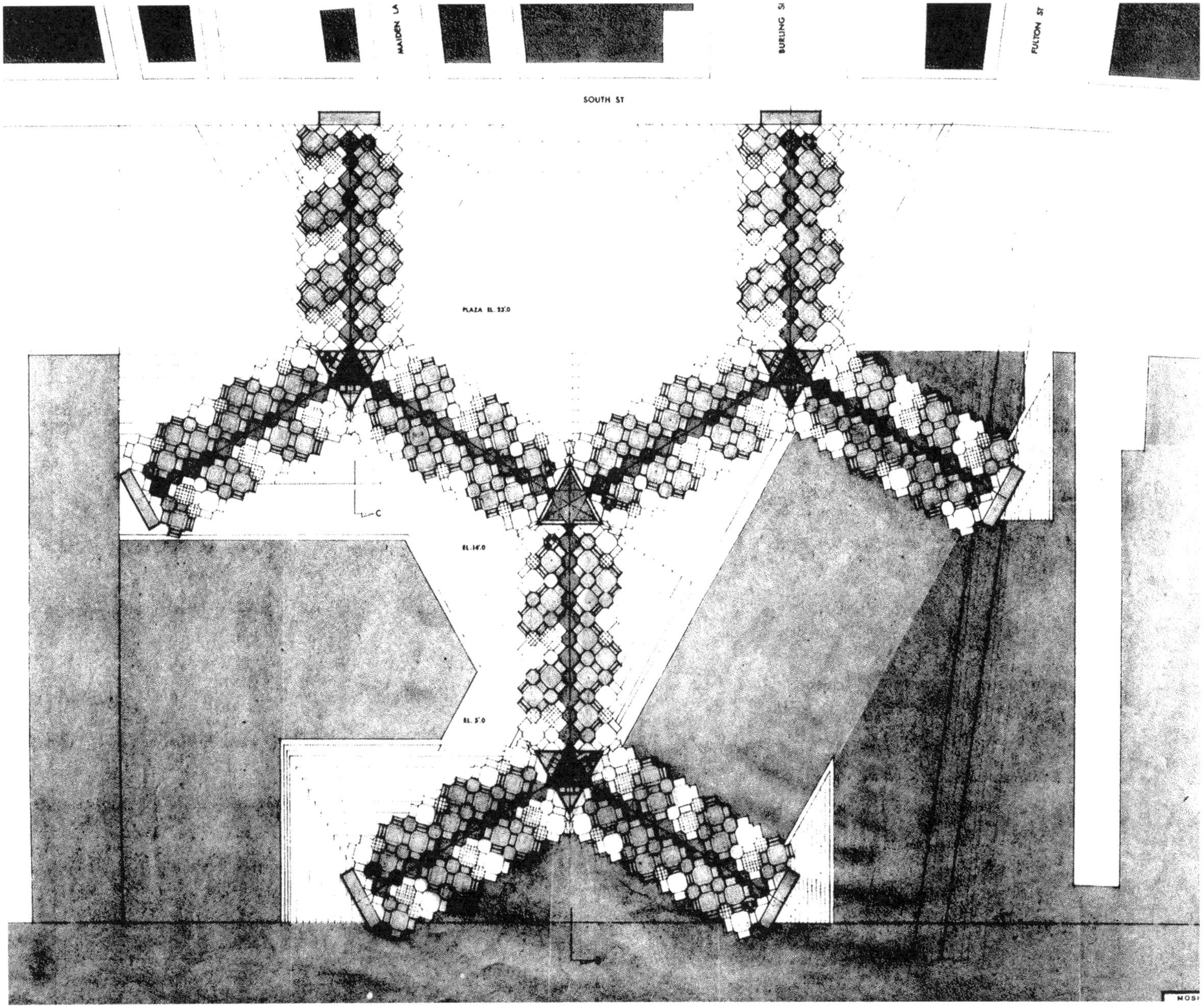

Site plan drawing, residential level, 1968

We didn't work out every detail, but conceptually there was an answer. It's a robust structure. The units didn't have to be concrete—they could be a lightweight enclosure. The client was very naive—very close to Mayor Lindsay—who promised to deliver a Habitat for New York, which the mayor was very excited about. I don't even remember exactly why it didn't go forward.

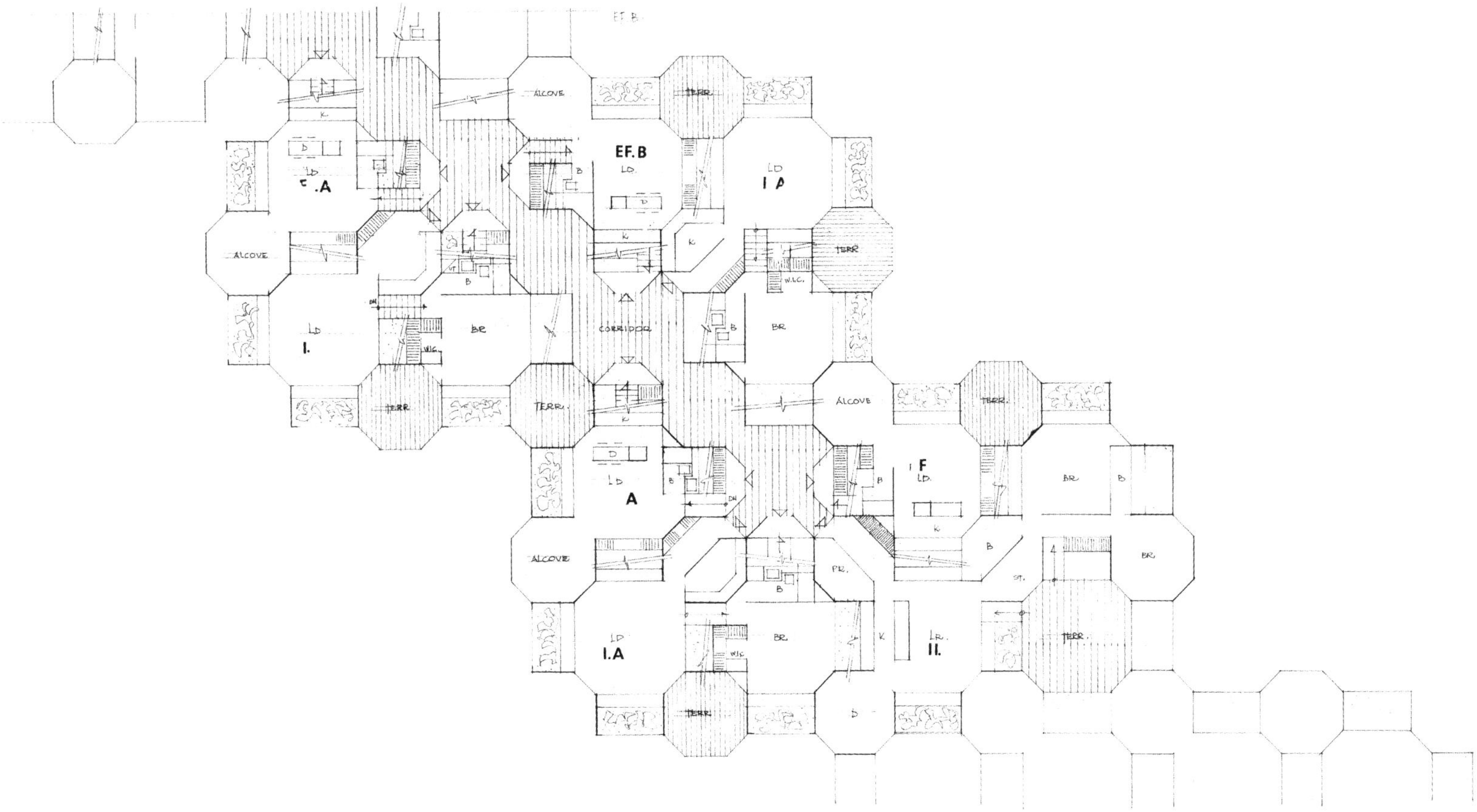

Plan detail drawing, residential layouts, 1968

Above: Model; photograph from "Global Citizen" exhibit, National Academy of Design (2015)

Right: Model; photograph from "Global Citizen: The Architecture of Moshe Safdie" exhibit, Boston Society of Architects (2016)

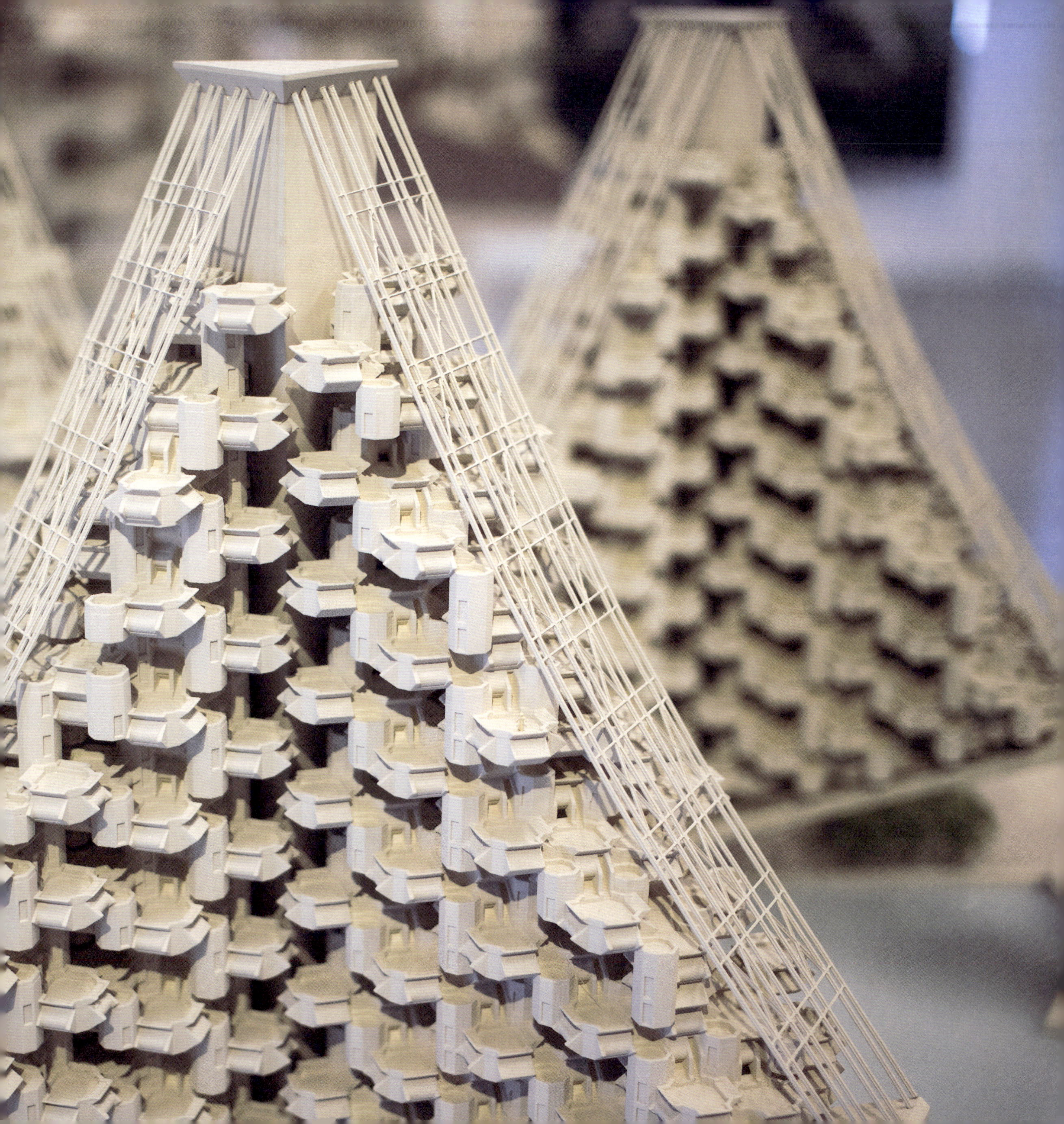

Pompidou Centre

Paris, France
1971

This competition entry for a major cultural center was produced in conjunction with a Yale School of Architecture studio. The center's program includes a national library, museums, theaters, restaurants, and cafés, as well as a station for high-speed trains connecting to the metropolitan region. The center is conceived as two inclined planes cantilevered from the sidewalk across the center of the block. On one corner the pedestrian sees terraces of glass and greenery—a public park accessible from the street. On the opposite corner the whole sheltered super-space is visible, with façades of nearby hotels forming the enclosing walls of the complex. Glass walls and roofs allow light directly into the lower levels and invite views to and from the surrounding streets. The structural system is based on a flexible grid, from which two cantilevered membranes are constructed using triangulated lattice structures.

Cross-section drawing, ink on vellum, 1971

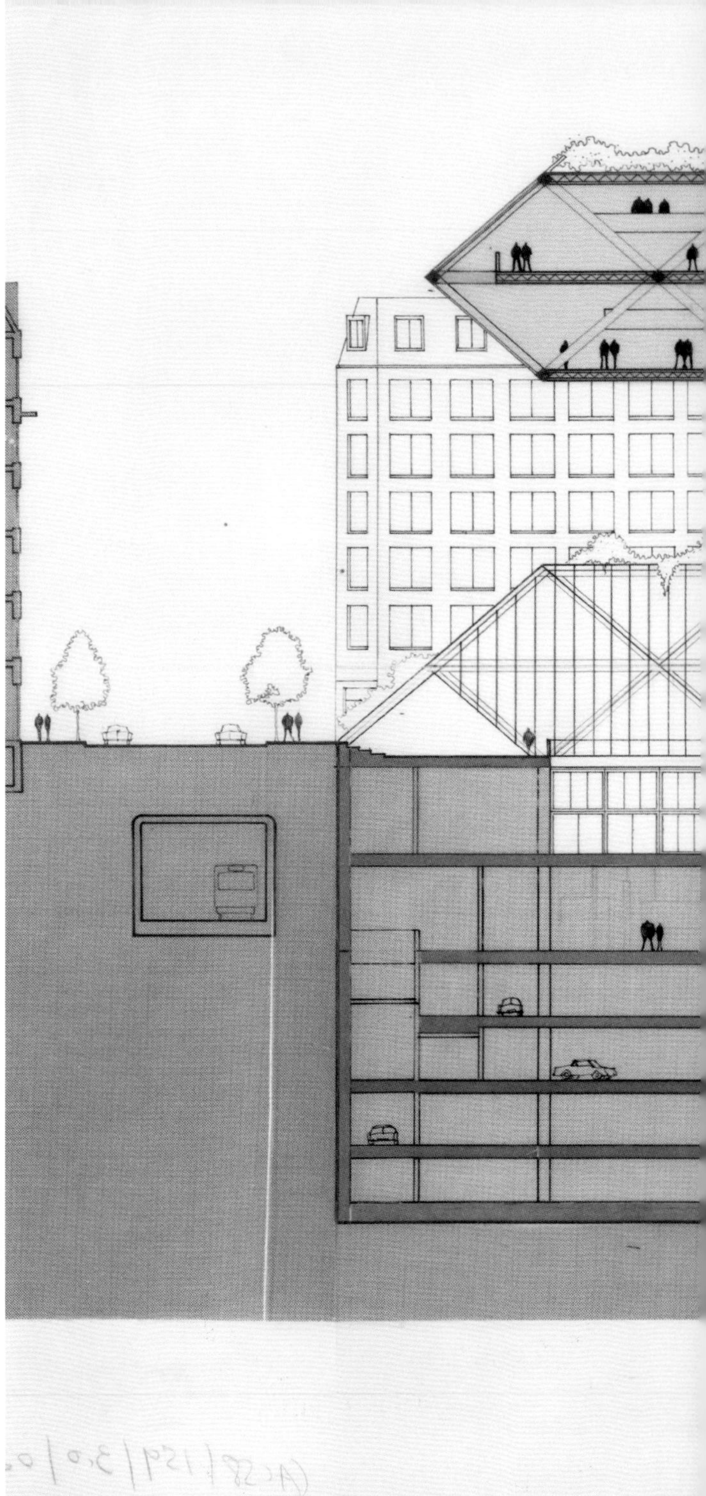

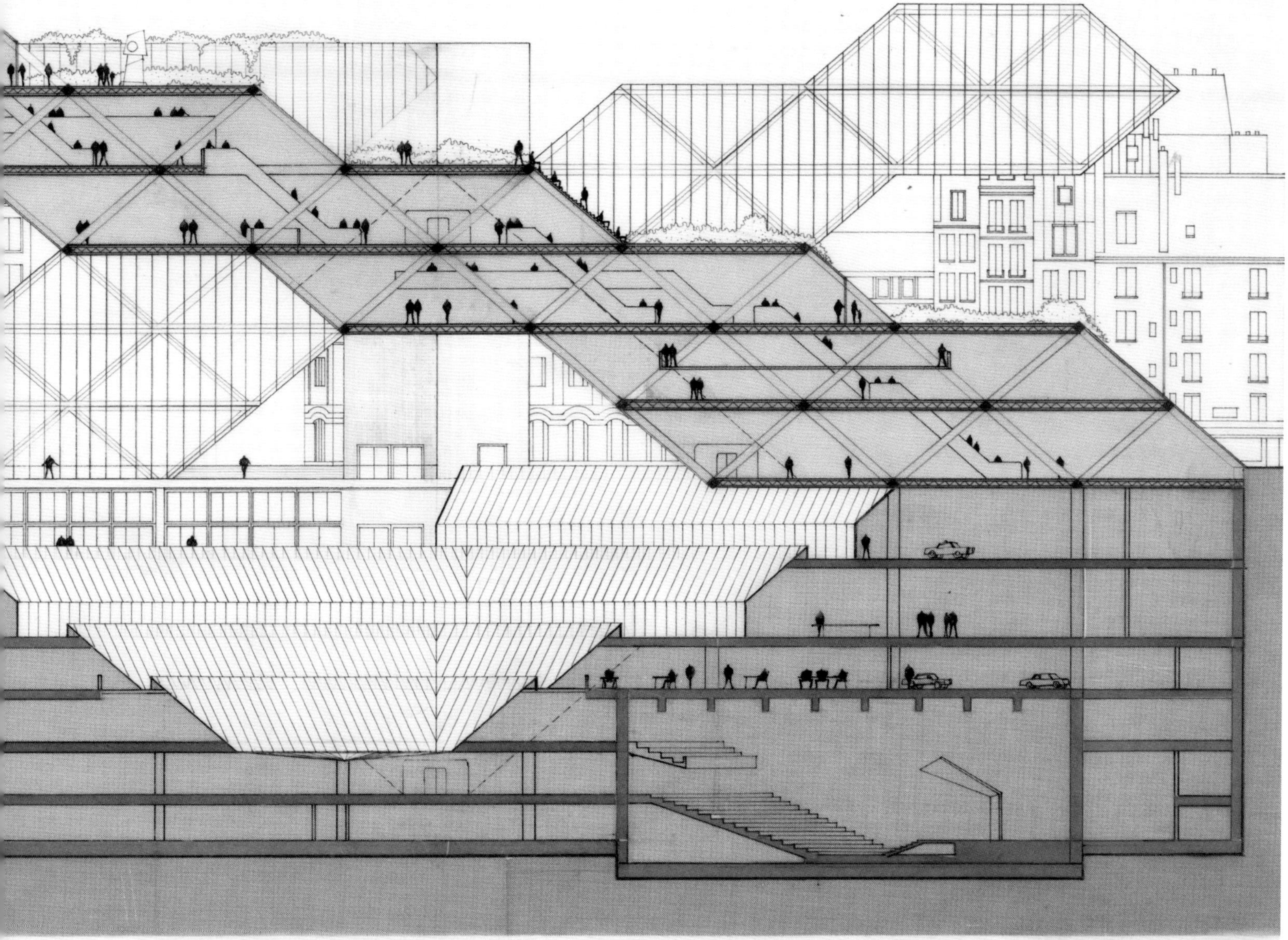

SECTION B–B

Model, 1971

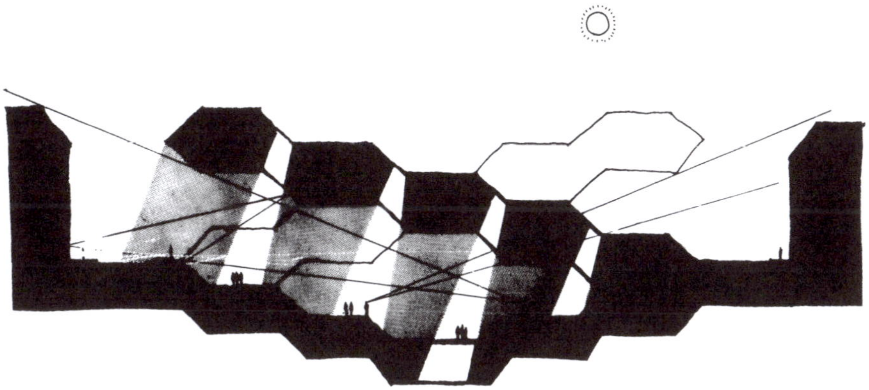

Diagrammatic section drawing, shading and views, 1971

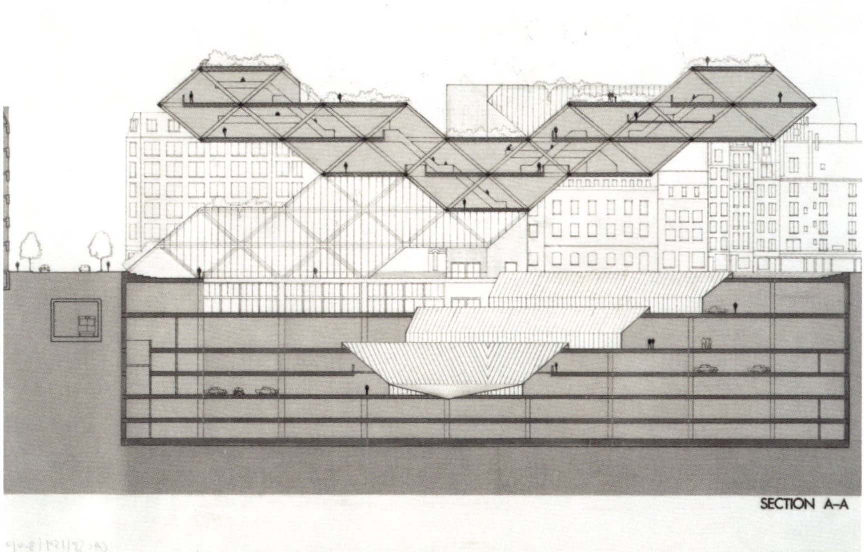

Cross-section drawing, ink on vellum, 1971

The design for the Pompidou Centre, which was awarded second place, pushes the idea of a building in which one can inhabit all of its surfaces—how does this theme extend through your architecture?

For me, the origins of that are the temples of Chichen Itza in the Yucatán and other buildings you climb on. The ground plane extends into the building. They are objects in space with extensions of the ground plane. Sometimes they are hollowed out. At Pompidou, we took it a step further: not only can you walk under the building but the ground plane is part of the square around it. It brings it into the heart of the building as a space. The building hovers over a series of piazzas. It would be an amazing space, although it would need to be detailed and crafted properly. But it was no more challenging than Rogers and Piano's building.

The idea extends from Habitat.

Habitat, the Hanging Gardens of Babylon, even the pueblos with the ladders on the roof in the southwestern US and Mexico, which I visited in 1961 while on a traveling scholarship.

There were other projects that did that. There was a design for a student center for UCLA that I worked on for a year that did not get built, very much in the same spirit—climbable.

Model (competition entry; 46 x 34 x 16 inches H), 1971

Above: Model (competition entry; 46 x 34 x 16 inches H), 1971

Opposite: Model, photograph from *Global Citizen: The Architecture of Moshe Safdie* (2015), 2010

Model, photograph from *Global Citizen: The Architecture of Moshe Safdie* (2015), 2010

Digital renderings, 2019

Western Wall Precinct

Jerusalem, Israel
1971–1994

One of Jerusalem's holiest sites, the Western Wall is the remnant of Herod's second temple. A large plaza in front of the wall was formed in 1967 when structures were cleared to accommodate pilgrims. The plan was commissioned by the city and the Company for the Reconstruction and Development of the Jewish Quarter.

The prayer area is excavated to the Herodian street level, 30 feet below the terrain. The design creates public squares that terrace up from gathering places near the wall to the quarter's residential structures to the west. To the south, the ruins of an Umayyad palace are to be partly restored, including its grand stair. An arcaded street parallel to the wall separates sacred and secular traffic, tying Dung Gate to the markets. New plazas connect through a series of grand stairs descending from the upper city, improving access to the wall precinct from surrounding areas.

Collage/model, Scheme II, View from southwest toward Western Wall and Temple Mount, 1974

Model, Scheme I, 1972

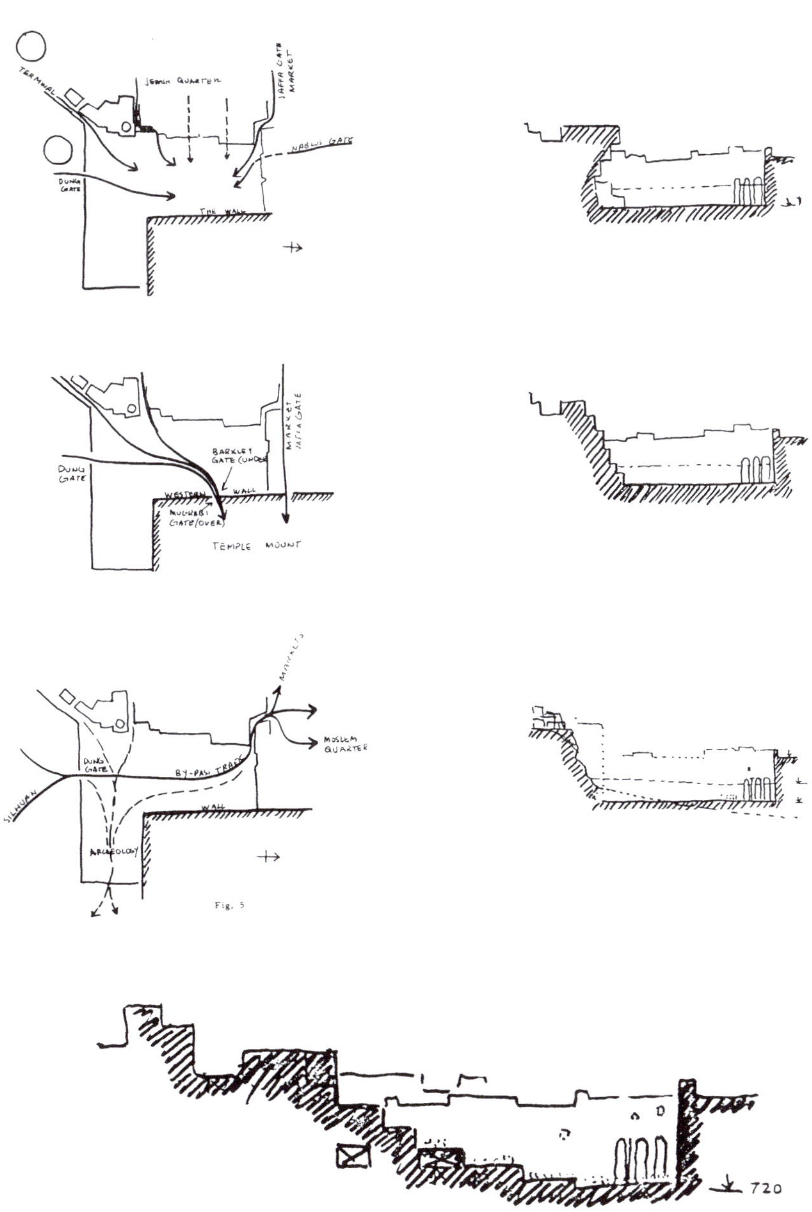

You've said that designing in Jerusalem, particularly the Western Wall project, made you more sensitive to the power of immediate context in design. How does the power of context reverberate through projects that followed it?

After relocating with my family to Montreal in 1953, I didn't go back to Israel for 19 years. I've always had affection for the vernacular of the Middle East. I remember visiting Arab villages, spending a lot of time in Jerusalem, doing sketches for a thesis design for the Knesset—a Sinan-like complex all under a big dome. I went back for a commission to restore part of the Jewish quarter and to design a major new building in the heart of the city.

They already had an American architect who had designed a glass box, and all hell broke loose. There was a big debate about the context and the modernists were saying you should just ignore it. It was my disposition not to ignore it.

Parti sketches, circulation diagrams and section drawings

A–A

Maybe if I was not Sephardic and didn't have an affinity for Middle East culture I might not have been as sympathetic. But it was transformative. Once I decided to solve it and build in stone, and explore how concrete could cohabitate with stone, it was transformative. It affected the next few commissions in Canada.

The first was the Musée de la civilisation in the old city of Quebec, then the National Gallery of Canada in Ottawa, both of which are strong attempts to dialogue with their traditional environment. Both would have been inconceivable for me before the experience of working in Jerusalem. The critics said, the precedent for the National Gallery is Bruno Taut's crystalline buildings, which is true, although I didn't know Taut's work at the time. To me, it was an attempt to harness the Gothic geometry of Ottawa to create a contemporary neo-Gothic language. At Skirball a few years later, it was my interpretation of California, the Spanish vernacular. Later on, this approach guided our work in India. It's about what can be divined from the place.

Section drawing, Western Wall complex

Model, Scheme I, 1972

Model, Scheme I, 1972

Sketch, ink and pastel
Sketchbook 43
Moshe Safdie, 1986

Supreme Court of Israel

Jerusalem, Israel
1985–1986

Poised on Jerusalem's highest hill, on axis with the Knesset (parliament) building, the Supreme Court competition design responds to the tradition of justice expressed in Psalm 85: "Truth rises from the earth, and justice reflects from heaven." A square compound is divided into a triangular forecourt to the south and a court building to the north. Limestone pillars rise 52 feet, inscribed with legal teachings from scriptures, holy books, and the annals of justice. The pillars create a shaded grove, a contemplative place. Overhead trellises form a pattern of light and shade, evoking the sukkah—a place of public gathering. Two intersecting glass roofs cover the courtrooms. At night, light from the court illuminates the inner shell. Rising above the evening skyline, the courtrooms join the light of justice with the lamps of government and religion, embodied in the Knesset, mosques, churches, and synagogues.

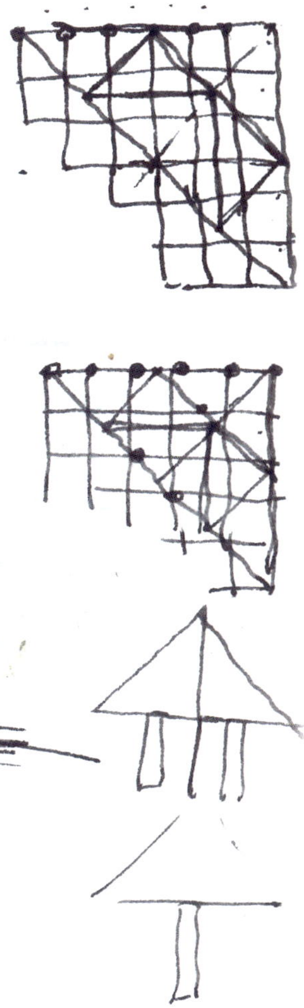

Model, 1986

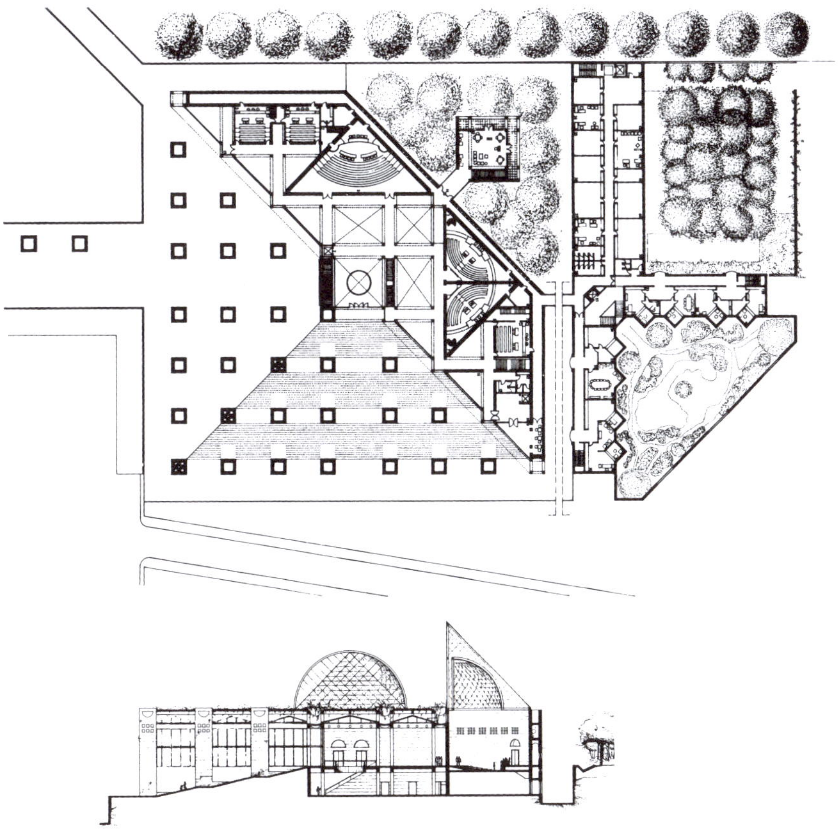

Site plan and east/west section drawings, 1986

The Supreme Court of Israel seems a design about transition and gathering, moving from outside to inside, and creating reflective exterior places that exude a sense of the pillars of law in a just society. How did that design reverberate through other projects, such as the Skirball Cultural Center?

The Supreme Court is a very romantic project. I say romantic because I got very involved in going back to the sources in the scriptures that dealt with justice and the court system. The informality of the courts was a recurring theme. The judges sat by the city gate and dispensed justice under the trees. There's no talk about palaces of justice. So there is a pervading informality, almost naturalistic, about the courts, yet the site called for a ritualistic response to governance and justice. The deployment of these massive columns, that seem archeological, and the tree-like roof are all very romantic. I think it would have appealed to people's sense of romanticism—they would have gotten it. On one hand there would be a sense of monumentality and permanence—carved out of rock, it's there forever. But at the same time there would be an informality

Sketch, pastel, Sketchbook 43
Moshe Safdie, 1986

that is very romantic. I don't think the design jury got it. It's too bad I never had the chance to present it, because I didn't get shortlisted. Which angered me. I rarely get angry when I lose a competition—I get disappointed, but not angry. I felt it was absurd. In some ways it put me off about Israel's attitude towards me, generally.

Talk about that.

The grass always looks greener. For example, [Alvar] Aalto was the national architect of Finland; he could do no wrong, the best commissions, great support in realizing them. You could say the opposite for me in Israel: everything I did came out of extraordinary struggle. Yeshiva Porat Yosef wasn't fully realized because of the terrible, corrupt rabbis; the Western Wall did not go forward because of many factors; Mamilla is built because I stuck with it tirelessly for 40 years, not because of any winds pushing on our sails. In some ways I have had extraordinary opportunities: doing an entire city like Modi'in, our first airport at Ben Gurion. But of all the competitions we did in Israel we never won one.

Above: Model, 1986

A prophet is not welcome in his own homeland.

That's particularly remembered by the Jews, who coined the phrase.

Opposite: Model, courtroom roofs, 1986

Sketch, ink and pastel, Sketchbook 48
Moshe Safdie, 1986

Digital rendering, 2018

Renderings, colored pencil, Michael Guran, 1986

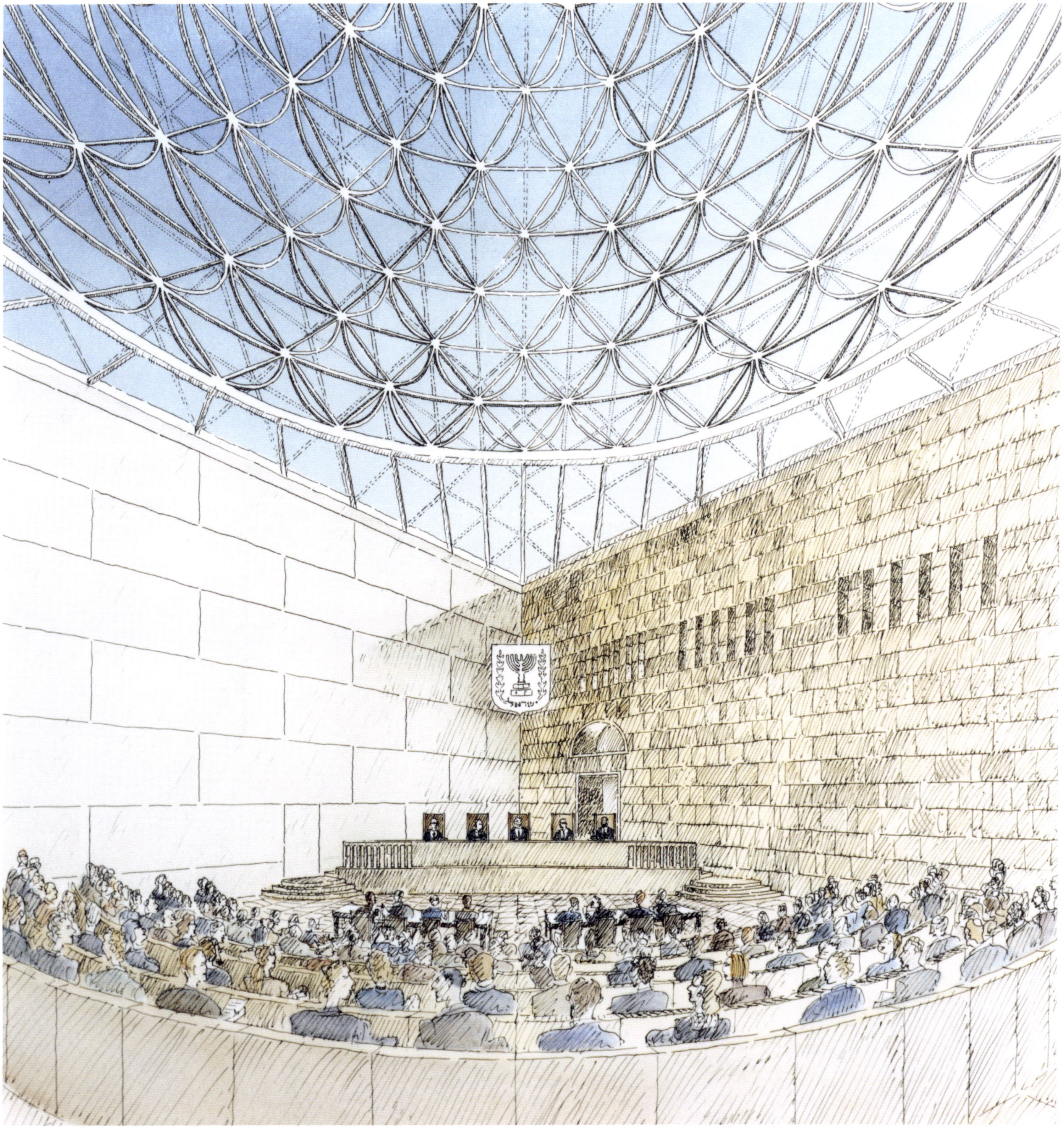

Columbus Center

New York, New York, USA
1985–1987

The Columbus Center design reinforces the civic image of the circle enhancing the life of the street. Set back in a V-shape, two towers surround a 190-foot-tall garden atrium. The towers' separation highlights the 59th Street axis and admits generous amounts of light. The towers are structurally independent but share horizontal forces through regularly spaced five-story braces. The towers, 62 and 69 stories, connect via a bridge at the 39th level and sit on a base enclosing a four-story atrium. A large public galleria follows the circle's curve.

Secondary tower-like facets in scale with Central Park West apartment towers form a transition between the urban scale of the Upper West Side and Midtown. Setbacks in the towers accommodate greenhouses that provide an amenity for the office workers and create a visual connection with Central Park.

The project halted after the withdrawal of Salomon Brothers as developer.

Collage/model photograph of view west on 59th Street; 1986

You conceived of Columbus Center as two towers tightly stitched at the street level into the pedestrian experience of the city. How has Columbus continued to influence your design of towers and their contribution to urban precincts?

Columbus was very site specific—a great square that faces the park and two subway stations. The natural tendency of the development program was to create a big shopping center that draws you off the street. Instead, I was asking: How can we get something like Vittorio Emanuele in Milan that goes from street to street, so much part of the movement on the street you don't even think of it.

The two subway stations helped—you could enter either side and move around the circle itself, giving you a natural path of movement. You would want large portals at either end and one at the center. What was built sort of does that, but not powerfully enough. We wanted to reinforce street life on the square by moving people along the circle. The trading floors on the upper levels were enormous, so we created a garden that hovers over the street and opens to it.

Above: Sketch, pastel on trace paper
Moshe Safdie, 1985

Opposite: Model, 1985

ESSEX
HOUSE

On the site, 59th Street used to go through so you can't put a tower on that axis. We were concerned about having to leave 10 Columbus Circle intact; that burdens the site a bit. These ideas got more and more complex in other dimensions in later projects such as Marina Bay Sands and Chongqing, where the scale is bigger and the opportunities for connecting to the city are more critical and numerous. In Chongqing we are literally at the crossroads of many paths, streets, and transportation systems that converge on the project.

Collage/model photograph of view over Central Park, 1985

Opposite: Section perspective drawing Great Hall and Galleria, 1985

Above: Rendering, colored pencil Interior view of Galleria, 1985

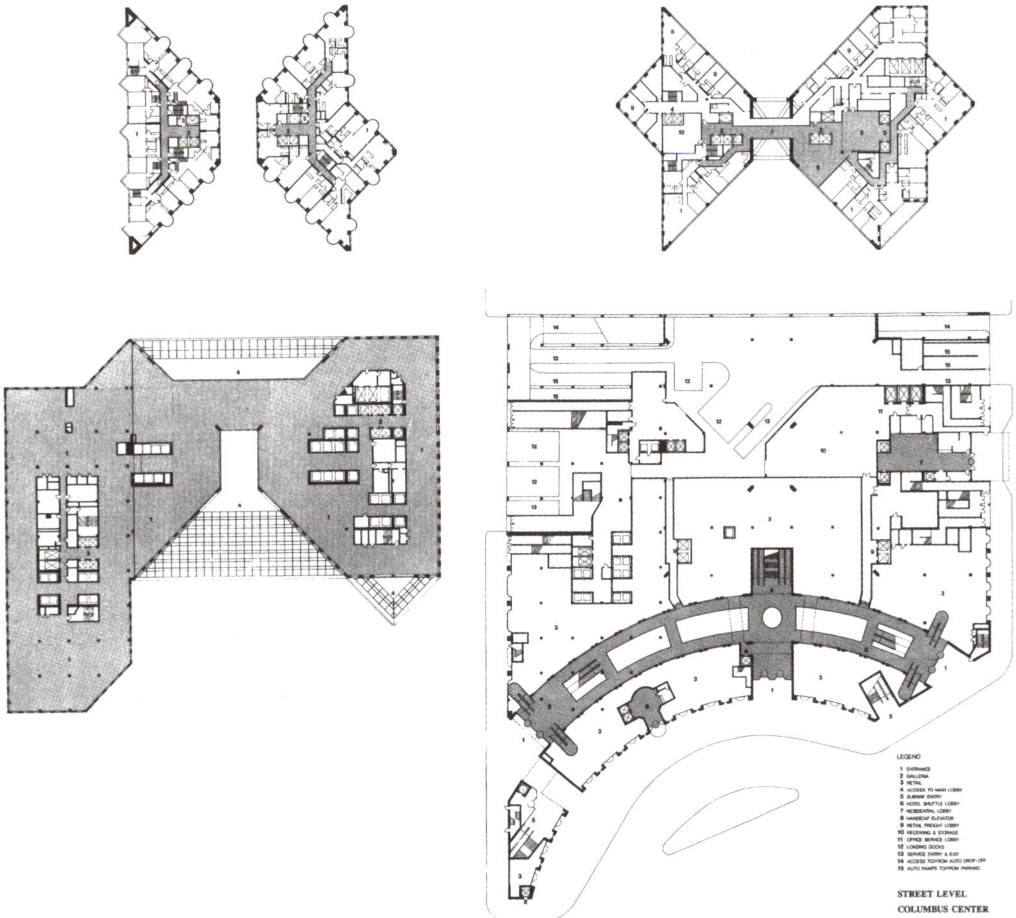

Above: Floor-plan drawings, residential, trading and street-levels, 1986

Right: Collage/model photograph of aerial view, 1986

GW

The skyline of America's cities is being transformed with dizzying speed by a rash of new skyscrapers born of corporate ego and post-modernism. Here, the doyenne of America's architectural critics explores the phenomenon

BY ADA LOUISE HUXTABLE

IN THE SHADOW OF THE ARCHITECT

The conventional name for a selective historicism is eclecticism; but the new eclecticism is not the orderly selection of elements from different styles and systems according to the established academic rules that marked its practice in the past. The new version of eclecticism is personal rather than institutional, to the point of being private, hermetic, and maverick all the way. The acknowledged leader of the skyscraper division of this kind of post-modern eclecticism is Philip Johnson, a man whose social and aesthetic credentials are impeccable and whose mercurial pursuit of a fast-moving avant-garde keeps the profession on its toes – or at least off balance – much of the time. His own work has moved from the sculptural abstraction of the IDS building in Minneapolis and Pennzoil in Houston to a picturesque eclecticism in which absolutely anything that can be copied or adapted goes, as long as it offers a constantly changing spectrum of sensations to an extraordinarily keen, responsive, and easily bored sensibility and mind. It must also be able to be blown up instantly to skyscraper scale.

LIKE A TURRETED CASTLE FOR MADISON AVENUE

The Johnson, Burgee firm offers a wide choice in its skyscraper line. The controversial Chippendale model for AT&T in New York, which made the cover of *Time*, putting architecture on the media map, was followed by medieval battlements in Lower Manhattan, a pinnacled mirror-Gothic highrise for PPG Industries in Pittsburgh, and a modernistic cylindrical tower in San Francisco. An occasional excess, like a turreted castle for New York's Madison Avenue, has been aborted, but the product has been popular, nationwide. These buildings trip lightly from style to style. Houston has the firm's Art Deco Transco tower and the new RepublicBank headquarters in the guise of a giant gingerbread guild hall. Clearly, the surface of history has only begun to be scratched.

If the sources are diverse, the results suffer from a certain sameness; rarely do these eclectic exercises coalesce into an architectural statement with the authority of the examples so blithely exploited. Their so-called playful use of history is heavy-handed; their paper-thin pretensions misfire, no matter how solidly enclosed or dazzlingly surfaced. But they do carry a message; their failure to capture the architectural importance that they aspire to through the use of samples and swatches selected at random from history is a demonstration of the essential and inescapable relationship between art and its generating forces, from structure to society. However, if cleverness can substitute for this confluence of formative factors, then these buildings are simply not clever enough. The problem is not that they fail to say the same thing as the buildings they crib from – that is neither possible in today's world nor their avowed intention – it is that they say nothing at all. The dumb but reasonably honest glass box at least has the virtue of a saving simplicity; there is no virtue in elaborate vacuity.

It becomes a point of wonder that such respected architectural devices as the arcades and oculi of the AT&T building, with the enormously exaggerated scale of the structure's traditionally composed base, shaft, and top, can result in anything so flaccid and so unexceptional as this assemblage of painstakingly and expensively executed details – tons of granite and pratfall playfulness notwithstanding.

The possibilities of cut-and-paste are endless. The immediate, and lasting, impression of the cardboard-like silhouette of the RepublicBank's "Flemish Gothic" top in Houston is that its tricky outline is an exasperatingly flat and lifeless *zigzag* against the sky. The Art Deco Transco tower, in the Post Oak neighbourhood – which like most Houston neighbourhoods is an invention rather than a place – is a better effort in part at least because it is based on a highly successful skyscraper prototype.

The developer who is the client for many of these structures, Gerald Hines of Houston, has found that rental response relates directly to a building's [illegible] identity and novelty give a builder a different product and a competitive edge. The size, importance and number of Hines's buildings in American cities has done a great deal to establish this increasingly familiar, commercially successful formula. But what is being sold is rarely architecture; it is a gimmick with a designer label. It is becoming a standard joke that some of the most dramatic details that suggest climactic views and spaces house mechanical equipment – an architectural put-on of consummate cynicism.

Hines uses other architects – I. M. Pei, and Skidmore, Owings, and Merrill, for example – although these architects still produce basically modernist, if somewhat loosened-up, buildings. It is the trickier, post-modern buildings that get the attention that translates into tenants and profits. If this level of sponsorship has predictable and sometimes pedestrian results, it is hard to blame a developer for staying with a sure thing rather than pursuing riskier architectural challenges. Hines's espousal of excellence has been a Sputnik-like breakthrough in a business known for its dedicated quest for new lows for the construction bottom line. At the same time, he describes his commitment in a revealingly candid way. "We do not collect architecture. We use it," he says. The limits of this kind of architectural patronage are clear.

If postmodern eclecticism is the answer to modernism, the battle of the styles has a long way to go. Instead of cookie-cutter modern, we are getting cookie-jar monuments. All are eye-catching and mind-boggling buildings and all raise serious architectural issues. Critical commentary, on the whole, has dealt with nothing more substantial than their silhouettes. The Johnson, Burgee work is clever costume design or scenography; one hesitates to call it architecture at all. More interesting is Johnson's aesthetic volatility; this early and ardent champion of the modernist revolution tak s pride in having been among the first to defect. What he favours now is the kind of style that Le Corbusier ridiculed as "the feather on a woman's head" in *Vers Une Architecture*, the slim volume published in 1923 that became the rallying cry for a generation that hoped to change the world. If irony is what the postmodernists want, there is plenty of it around. Their stand-up architectural one-liners have much more to do with fashion and merchandising than with style, and it is surprising how quickly the joke, and the impact, wear thin.

WE ARE GETTING COOKIE-JAR MONUMENTS

We are, then, at a most curious and contradictory moment, when the need for change and the craving for the familiar are claiming equal time and attention. Art must inevitably change; it is a dynamic force that moves with history if it is not to stagnate and die. Our desire for identity with an art that has meaning for our own time, at a universal level or at the level of our personal lives, is an enduring concern. Familiarity is reassuring, and identity, real or spurious, has an obvious appeal over anonymity. As we re-evaluate modernism it is natural and desirable to look at traditional models again, to seek touchstones of the past and to rediscover their values. What is peculiar – and peculiar to this moment – is the attempt to hybridize past and present in an unprecedented way, an effort that takes tremendous amounts of sophisticated knowledge, creative courage, and professional skill if it is to have any hope of success.

PUBLICITY IS MORE IMPORTANT THAN PRODUCT

Judgment of the new buildings, in terms of use, aesthetics, and environment, can be made only on completion and in context. They take enormous, conscious risks. The new freedom has created unparalleled opportunities and a time of dramatic promise and challenge. The bottom line is the critical question: What kind of architecture is being produced? Unfortunately, there seems to be little interest in answering it. Either out of genuine enthusiasm or a need to be with, and of, the new in art, few commentators are analyzing or evaluating the results with much critical objectivity. This, also, is not new; the role of club member or camp follower has always been more attractive than being considered out of it or incapable of understanding the new vision and values. And as has happened with so much of the art of our time, architectural criticism is becoming a game in itself, with an increasingly inaccessible language and a growing detachment from the built object. The buildings can hardly be seen for the words. Publicity is more important than the product.

It is hard not to see some of the most aggressively promoted examples of postmodernism, hailed as architectural breakthroughs, as surprisingly thin and inconsequential buildings. A do-it-yourself, kit-of-parts eclecticism turns the promise of revived grandeur into a paper-dollhouse architecture of plastic and plywood pilasters, and pediments and sheet-rock cut-outs. There is too much that is too cute, pretending to be erudite or clever. Personal stylistic statements are preferred to optimum solutions.

The conflict between function and expression is not new either; this is a legitimate, historic condition of architecture, and the manner in which the necessary equilibrium is achieved is intrinsic to the quality of the result. But the trade-off today is increasingly

Philip Johnson's notorious Chippendale-topped AT&T tower put post-modernism on the media map: it made the front page of the New York Times *and* the cover of Time magazine. Flanked to the left by the brash Trump tower, and to the right by the Citicorp building, it changed Manhattan forever

Moshe Safdie's proposal twin towers of offices, shops and flats at Columbus Circle, overlooking Central Park (left and above), isn't as tall as Donald Trump's alternative, but it's still enormous

20 Blueprint November 1986

Blueprint November 1986 21

Left: Cartoon by James Stevenson, first published in *The New Yorker* November 23, 1987

Above: "In the Shadow of the Architect" by Ada Louise Huxtable, first published in *Blueprint* magazine, November 1986

Architect's Response
Moshe Safdie

New York Times, November 8, 1987

To the Editor:

In "Square Deal for Columbus Circle?" [Oct. 18] , Paul Goldberger is critical of the size of Columbus Center, but also in the few lines devoted to the architecture, he terms the design ghastly, vulgar and pathetic.

There is more to architectural criticism than personal taste. In question are fundamental philosophical issues confronting architecture generally and the appropriate skyscraper design specifically.

My design does not fit into Goldberger's favored post-modern mold. It does not step back symmetrically; it does not have a templelike top, nor any classical recall. Rather, it attempts to relate to the site, and to evolve forms which are responsive to contemporary life in tall buildings.

The case is addressed in an editorial in the September issue of *Architettura*, written by Bruno Zevi, its editor in chief. Mr. Zevi has written scores of books on architecture and is one of the world's leading figures in architectural history and criticism. [The editorial said, in part:] "Moshe Safdie acquired international fame 20 years ago when, immediately after getting his degree, he built Habitat for the Montreal International Expo in 1967. At that time, Safdie proposed an alternative, loaded with creative potential, both to the widespread dispersion of suburban houses and urban apartment buildings and to the compact quality of Corbusian horizontal macrostructure. This complex interweaving of residential and service cells, based on an open scheme which is able to answer to the varying demands of growth and contraction, caught the attention of architects who were sensitive to the need of reaching beyond the gigantic boxlike volumes of Le Corbusier's Unite d'Habitation in Marseilles and Nantes.

"During these past two decades, Safdie has been trying to apply his wonderfully inventive idea in various contexts, yet with results of varying success. His language seemed to have remained trapped within the realm of a 'contemporary vernacular' without much potential.

"Now, on the other hand, we witness a new inventive leap: The subversion of the traditional skyscraper by means of a heretic grouping of tall structures designed for the new Columbus Center in New York.

"The program stated by the competition of 1985 included the enlargement of the existing office space on the southwest corner of Central Park, between Broadway and 58th Street, with the addition of a hotel, restaurants, residential space and public spaces crossed by a commercial galleria. Rather than proposing an isolated tower, placed without a reason in a nondescript point of the urban fabric, Safdie designed a complex and articulated structure; a conglomeration of fragments responding to the specific characteristics of function and place.

"Two asymmetrical towers of 58 and 69 floors rise up almost like springs from the interlocking of dissonant volumes which are in constant dialogue and resonance with different panoramic views.

"Moreover, the composite and segmented skyline of Columbus Center has been studied and designed so as to not encumber the horizon with a monolithic presence and so as to not cast long shadows on the park and on the surrounding streets. Everything has been calculated according to the movement of the sun; and, by night, the building glows with the many greenhouses that are scattered throughout, engaging the atrium and the suspended gardens as well.

"It is a refusal of the classicizing tendencies and of the academic compromises of post-modern architecture; a real ethical provocation which Safdie has launched with his usual courage. Of course, we are faced with a multitude of dissenting reactions; no to the dimensions; no to the cost; no to the 'esthetic prejudice.' A committee presided over by Jacqueline Kennedy Onassis was formed with the aim to stop the construction of this skyscraper. What can one do?

"In the middle of the 19th century, George Sand observed, 'The world is paved with idiots; you cannot make a step forward without hearing some scream.' The situation is not substantially different. Safdie's gripping and prophetic message underlines its vitality, reproducing in the vertical dimension Habitat's anomalous gesture and arousing, once more, a conservative storm."

Intensive negotiations are currently under way that are likely to result in a reduction in the size of the project. The city is receptive to new financial arrangements. But the issue here is architecture and our ability to move forward from the current mood of historic mimicry and fashionable exterior decoration to designs that aim to create a more humane and livable vertical city.

MOSHE SAFDIE
New York City

Skyscraper Shouldn't Look Down on Humanity
Moshe Safdie

New York Times, Architecture/ Design Section,
May 29, 1988

"We feel that postmodern ism is over. For projects which are going to be ready in five years, we are now considering new architectural appointments." So I was told by a major United States developer recently. He said it as a matter of course, with the naturalness of a clothing manufacturer who tells you that he does not want to be stuck with a line of blue coats when red is in.

Two weeks later I was talking to a developer in Montreal, planning a major downtown project. A large model was on display: out of a base formed by granite columns rose a tower, stepping back symmetrically, its upper portion crowned by a great copper pyramid supported by yet another columnar space. I made a sound of exclamation to which he responded, "Don't look at that. It's post-modern and post-modern is out."

To an architect charged with the design of a tall building, the agenda is indeed confusing. A design grows from a set of objectives. If the objective is to satisfy a short-term fashionability, then one must make sure of being up to date on the latest fads and public tastes.

But if one believes, as I do, that architecture has to do with the timeless and that the objectives for the design are founded in a building's purpose, a broader set of issues must be considered.

One might begin by examining tall buildings built in the recent and not so recent past. There are the early examples of Chicago and New York skyscrapers, when Louis Sullivan and his contemporaries first become fascinated with the possibilities of elevators, steel construction and the stacking of efficient and compact work space.

Alternatively, one might look to the more familiar and charming examples of historically inspired buildings of the early century. Though tall buildings were without historic precedent, it was natural for the architects of that period to seek inspiration in temples and palazzos, cathedrals and chateaux. Buildings were designed with bases, middles and tops. Architects drew on past styles: neoclassical, Gothic, Oriental. These buildings make abundantly clear that they were designed from the outside in. Little attention was given to the tall building as a working or living environment. The emphasis was on ornament, proportion, imagery, the soaring Gothic or the more ponderous neoclassical, focusing on appearance and composition as externally applied elements.

Not much changed with the advent of modernism. As the sleek glass and steel towers emerged, one would have assumed that a new approach was at hand. But for all the modernists' fascination for transparency, lightness, and minimalist abstract forms, their designs of tall buildings were fundamentally the same: abstract compositions designed from the outside in. This approach is manifested in theoretical projects, such as Le Corbusier's Cruxiform Towers of Ville Radieuse and Mies van der Rohe's rounded glass towers, as well as realized in such buildings as the Unite d'Habitation apartment block in Marseilles and the Seagram's tower in New York.

Today we come full circle to post-modernism only to discover that this reaction to modernism was also primarily stylistic. The spice of life, missing in modernist designs, was to be achieved through externally applied decoration.

When applied to houses and museums, post-modernism, at its best, rekindled an interest in regional architecture and the importance of context. The application of post-modernism to tall buildings led to a further dehumanization of the building environment. The application of post-modernism to tall buildings led to a further dehumanization of the building environment. For tall buildings ushered yet another chapter in grand styling, devoid of any relationship with livability and fit into the city. A great alliance was forged between the world of real estate developers, advertising and corporate merchandising with a new breed of architects who could respond with memorable, eye-catching, novel tall buildings. The merchandisers were quick to realize how easy it was to achieve a readily marketable product of great promotional value by means of a skin-deep styling treatment of buildings. Such an approach did not interfere with or change the basic, profitable formula for tall buildings: larger and larger floor plates with efficient and cheaper skins (curtain walls) for offices, and closely compacted apartments for residential buildings. With minimum investment—decorative skin patterns, elaborate tops and sometimes bottoms—one could achieve the appearance of a varied and rich architecture.

In a recent lecture to a well-informed New York audience, I flashed slides of familiar tall buildings, except that their bases and tops were masked off. I suggested a quiz: who could name the buildings? There was silence in the room as one familiar building after another defied identification.

As critics praise or attack specific designs according to their varied tastes, a rapid deterioration in the quality of the working and living environment in tall buildings is occurring. The change is quantitative: more of us work and live in tall buildings every year. It is also qualitative: office buildings are increasingly large, and rely on mechanical ventilation. Fewer people have the benefit of windows or the sight of daylight or views. The internal working environment is ever more alienating and suppressive. Gloomy office landscapes are contained within the glittering facades.

If you happen to live in the tall building you do not fare much better. Smaller in space, with depressing corridors, minimal fenestration, the modern apartment is lagging farther and farther behind a traditional house in quality of life.

Nor has the fit of tall buildings into their urban or suburban context improved as mixed-use tall buildings have emerged. Such buildings often contain major shopping facilities in their lower levels with offices and apartments above, as in the case of the John Hancock Building in Chicago, the Trump and Olympic Towers in New York, and more recently in the proposed Columbus Center. Mixed-use tall buildings multiply the risks of the exterior-decoration approach. Now diverse uses are forced into simplistic, externally preconceived envelopes, and large shopping atria are placed introvertly within projects, turning their backs on city streets and creating oases for the privileged.

Twenty-five years ago I proposed rethinking the apartment building from first principles. People preferred houses to apartments. They liked entering through streets, with recognizable entrances, windows that faced many ways, gardens in which to sunbathe and barbecue, and privacy. Could one, within realistic economic boundaries, provide these qualities in a tall building? The result: Habitat '67 at Expo in Montreal, a building that looked like no tall building built before it, appearing more like a hilltown than an orderly palazzo. As the years passed, I became obsessed with the more complex and demanding problem of the working environment in tall buildings.

Others have explored other aspects: Kevin Roche in the Ford Foundation introduced the interior garden as a humanizing element for offices. Louis Kahn, in his theoretical studies, and Norman Foster, in the Hong Kong Bank, both explored ways structure can be articulated to give scale and become a building's ornament.

I considered Columbus Center's mixed-use program an ideal laboratory to explore these ideas. The building contained all the ingredients: large public spaces with shops and theaters, an enormous concentration of office space and apartments above. The public shopping spaces take the form of a great curved galleria, linking the glass-covered garden they open onto with the surrounding city streets. They were an extension of the street system and by their presence animated the entire district. They were—in their scale, materials and accessibility—truly public, in the tradition of the great European gallerias of the 19th century. To enhance the environment in the offices at the lower levels of the building where thousands of people would work without benefit of view, the building was carved out to form a garden that was oriented to the morning and afternoon sun. As the offices ascended, the facades articulated to benefit from sun and views. The apartments stepped back, forming a hilltown with greenhouses, terraces and suspended glass rooms—dwelling units with multiple orientations and places to enjoy nature.

The building's appearance, its *style*, evolved and expressed each of these elements—not a singular decorated mass but a varied expression of its many uses. The imagery was of hanging gardens, the antithesis of the simplified templelike composition. Structural bracing became an element that broke down the scale. The dual towers are made up of a series of clustering mini-towers were made up of a series of clustering mini-towers that echoed the scale of the Upper West Side, minimized the mass and proclaimed by their diversity that so large a building was not a singular element but a macrocosm of the city.

The term "style" brings us to the crux of the matter. Is style a preconceived visual pattern borrowed from the past without regard to the purpose of a building; or worse, as in fashion, an arbitrary visual manipulation appealing to an idiosyncratic and insecure society controlled by the world of merchandising? The different attitudes to style are manifested in two recent books about tall buildings. Paul Goldberger's *The Skyscraper* (1981) reflects the popularly held view of design and style: It outlines the brief history of tall buildings as one would review the evolution of fashion in the garment industry. The fundamental connection of the roots and source of style—the tall building as a living and working environment—remains in the background. Style is there for its own sake; the grand game of making sculpture at the urban scale.

In contrast, in her 1982 book *The Tall Building Artistically Reconsidered*, Ada Louise Huxtable says: "The exploration of *style* can and does enlarge the boundaries of art; but in architecture, it also creates a special danger. Style detached from the conditions and considerations upon which the art of building rests can reduce architecture to something less than its proper role and definition . . . a necessary attachment to reality. This emphasis not only affects the use and value of architecture to society, it ultimately and tragically diminishes it as an art." Commenting on the array of recent post-modern designs, she continues: "But history should teach reasonable and profound lessons about the use of style. It should not be used to supply obscure illusions or decorative ready-mades . . . Preoccupation with surface appears to be coupled with a sheer stubborn disregard for the people and cities the structures serve."

Beyond its own form, the tall building challenges us with a problem of how it fits into its urban setting with little precedent to go on. Neither the nineteenth century gridded city nor its Renaissance and medieval predecessors anticipated the problems of concentration that the tall building imposes. The first gut reaction of the urban theorists early in the century was to place them far apart from each other. The resulting Ville Radieuse of towers set in parkland and its many derivatives resulted in a death blow to urbanism: unworkable cities, streets for traffic and alienated pedestrians. In its most extreme manifestation, in new cities like Houston, unburdened by zoning and urban history, we are presented with the frightening dimension of this surrealistic dream. At the opposite end of the scale, within the existing street patterns of New York and Chicago, Boston and Philadelphia, we have permitted the indiscretion of vertical multiplication of buildings to the extent of 15 to 20 times the area of the land they occupy. Here, connection becomes congestion and the striving for continuity results in a density that insults our sensibilities.

The tall building humanistically reconsidered calls for a new agenda for its design, and with equal urgency, the necessity for defining appropriate densities and concepts at street level. It is the tragedy of the campaign of the various New York groups against the size of Columbus Center (as well as that of other projects) that it diverts attention from the real issue: the prevailing densities of central Manhattan. It is ridiculous on one hand to support a density of 15 times the land area (plus additional density through bonuses granted in exchange for public improvements) for all of midtown while attacking individual projects. The particular sites, being larger and more open, are capable of supporting greater densities than the surrounding areas. The density at Columbus Center, or Television City for that matter, might burden the infrastructure of Manhattan, but the many uncontested towers rising in full conformity with midtown zoning on Second, Third, Madison and Seventh Avenues form a greater threat to the quality of life in the city than these particular projects. What we need is a general down-zoning, making it possible for tall buildings to be designed more humanely, for streets to be better placed, and for new development to be forced into the underutilized and underbuilt sections of the city and the region.

The zoning should encourage, indeed mandate, bases for tall buildings that form a continuous animated street facade. They should forbid internal atria and shopping centers that turn their backs on the city streets. The more slender towers resulting from reduced densities could rise above their bases at some reasonable distance from each other. Mixed-use towers should be encouraged, as they lead to a more rational massing and improved amenities. Down-zoning should be accompanied by a rethinking of the bonus system. It has proven to be too costly a method of financing public improvements. The system of artificially appreciating the value of the land so that part of the gain can be directed to public improvements has led to dubious improvements at a high public cost.

Eighty years is a very short period for the evolution of a brand-new building type. It took hundreds of years for temples, cathedrals, palaces—indeed towns and cities—to evolve in the past. In that context we must recognize that the architecture of the tall buildings, their appropriate form and style, are yet to emerge. The last 80 years represents merely a flirtation with the issue; an innocent extension of the experience of thousands of years of low-rise buildings. That evolution will be advanced only by an architectural philosophy that has as its most fundamental concern the quality of life of those who inhabit the buildings and the cities in which those buildings are set.

Ballet Opera House

Toronto, Canada
1987–1990

The site for the project is downtown, near a subway to increase access by public transport. The new theatre is planned like a micro-city, asymmetrical in form. At the northeast corner near the subway, stage entrances lead to a glazed corridor—the Gallery of the Artists, a high-arched ramped colonnade. This is the spatial backbone of the design, providing an interface between the ballet/opera companies and the general public—an urban street with shops, a library, lecture room, and the ballet/opera boutique. The horseshoe-shaped auditorium accommodates 2000 seats and is surrounded by six levels of round-arched loggias, reminiscent of traditional theaters in Europe. The auditorium roof is crowned by a glazed dome and triangular-based pyramid. Precast concrete panels inlaid with marble and granite compose the exterior, in scale with the surrounding streets. The interplay of natural/artificial light and glazing/solid walls results in a rich architectural vocabulary.

Model, competition scheme, 1988

Let's talk about the Ballet Opera House.

There's politics for you.

It seems to draw together several design imperatives—the connection to infrastructure and the importance of daylight. How did it influence the design of later projects?

In some ways, in terms of the roofs and the skylights, it was informed by the Supreme Court. Also the National Gallery—the great ramp where you move through the building before you enter. The opera hall is very much part of the horseshoe tradition of halls. I think in many ways it's the least contemporary building we've ever done. It draws on traditional ritual, the use of rich materials on the interiors.

It was also a new idea, a ballet/opera house, bringing two companies together, with rehearsal rooms and workshops on the street so you could see art in the making, bringing the community into it.

Sketch, ink and pastel on trace paper
Moshe Safdie, 1988

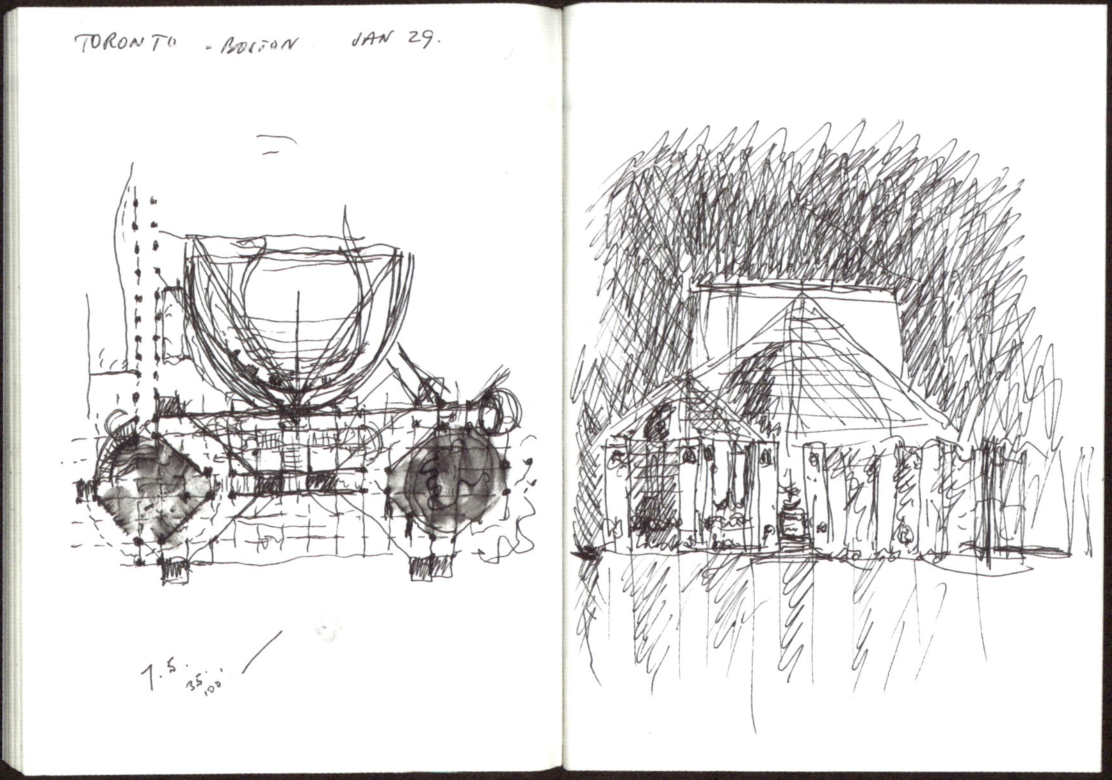
TORONTO - BOSTON JAN 29.

Feb 7. 88

Opposite top: Sketch, ink, Sketchbook 50
Moshe Safdie, 1988
Opposite bottom: Sketch, ink and pastel,
Sketchbook 51, Moshe Safdie, 1988

Above: Model, 1988

Above: Model, interior view, 1989

Right: Sketch, ink and pastel
Sketchbook 63, Balustrade studies
Moshe Safdie, 1990

Model, interior view
Auditorium study, 1988

Model (final design)
1989

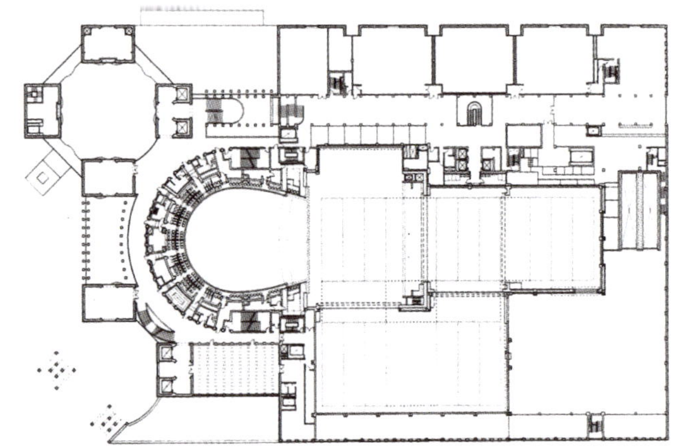

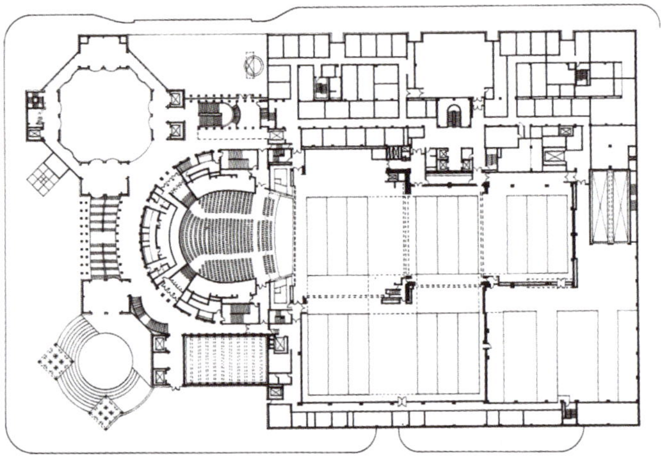

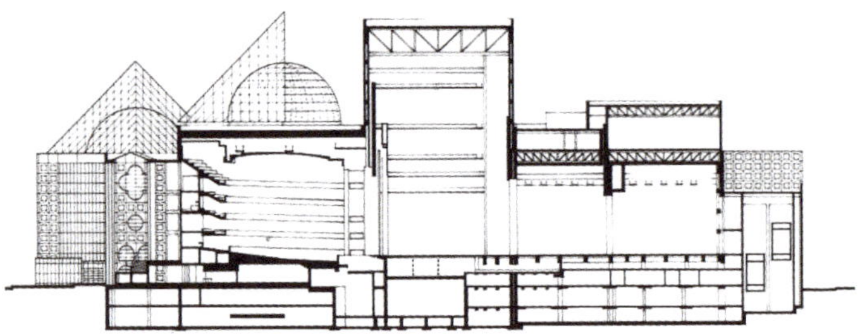

Above: Floor-plan and section drawings (final design), 1989

Right: Model (final design), 1989

Museum of Contemporary Art Stuttgart

Stuttgart, Germany
1990

Designed for a site amid historic and cultural institutions, the museum forms a gateway to downtown and marks the beginning of the city's cultural and civic core. The design program includes permanent galleries as well as temporary galleries that can be designed and built according to changing exhibit needs. The permanent galleries constitute the museum's urban spine, organized in two groups: one arranged as a series of "houses," the other vertically stacked as a tower. Possible configurations such as pyramidal, sky-lit large rooms, narrow rooms with saw-tooth skylights, black boxes, or egg-shaped galleries of translucent material demonstrate the design's versatility. With the giant crane, temporary galleries can be moved and transferred to off-site storage. When not in use, the crane is a motionless spire, then transforms itself into a dynamic symbol of change as it swings to position new artworks or convert temporary galleries.

Model, 1990

Sketch, ink and pastel

Sketchbook 69, Moshe Safdie, 1991

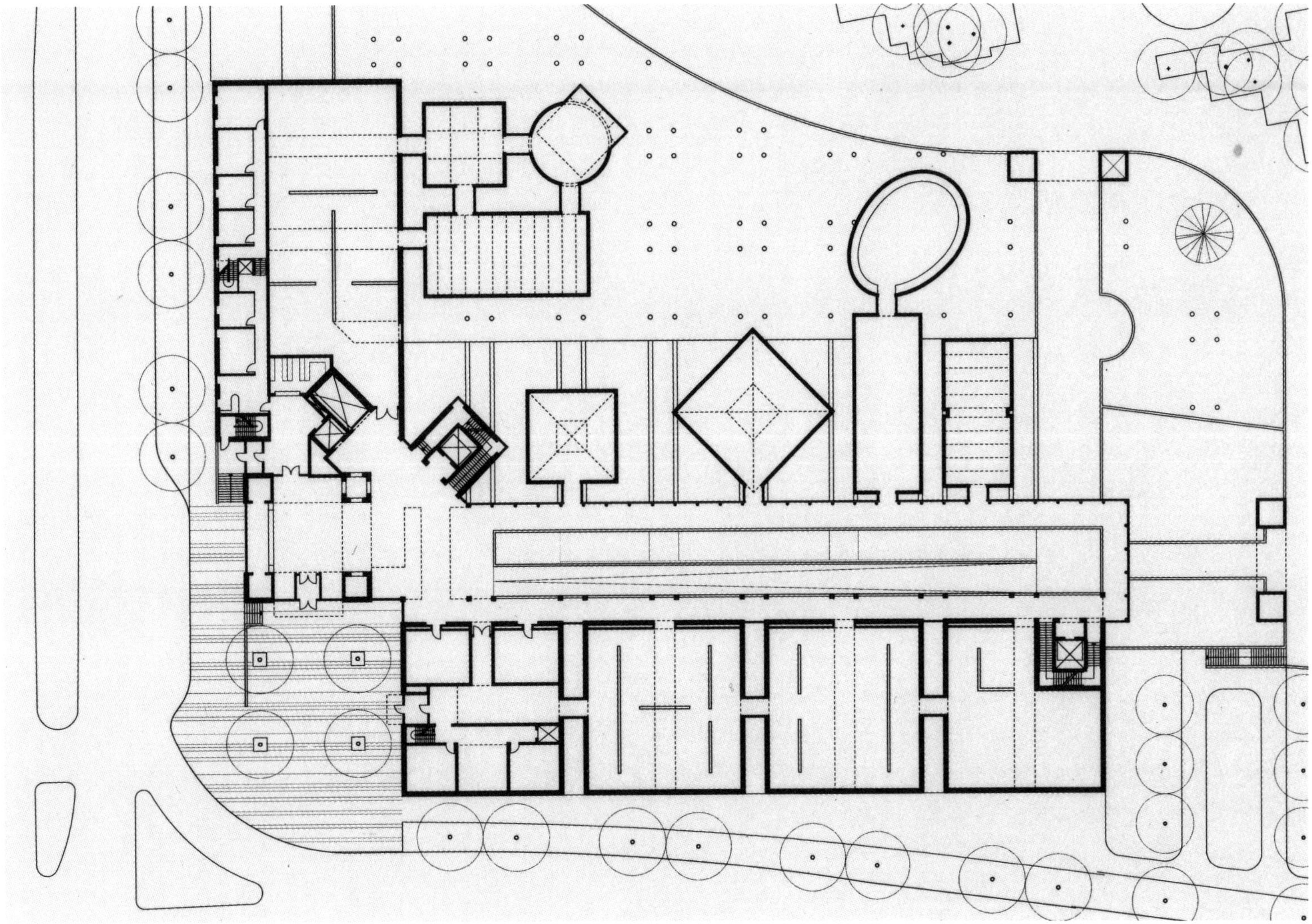

Floor-plan drawing,
ink on mylar, 1990

Model, movement of crane, 1990

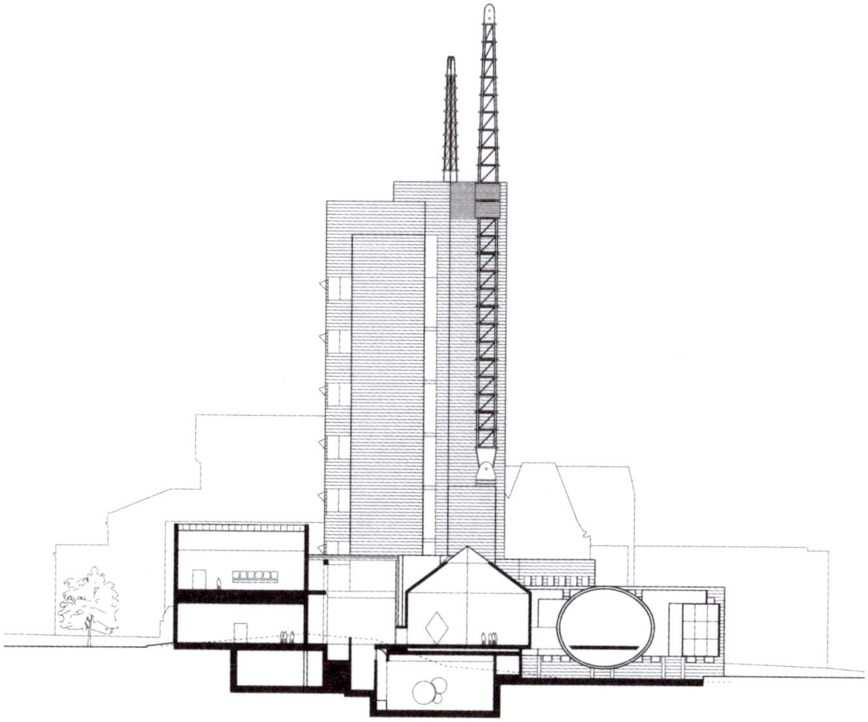

Cross-section drawing, permanent and movable galleries, 1990

In the Museum of Contemporary Art in Stuttgart, we see formalistic premonitions of the design of the Peabody Essex Museum. But what about the idea of a building in motion, constructing and deconstructing? Is that an idea that has surfaced in your architecture over the years?

I think the idea of pavilions with the light coming between them to the galleries goes back to the National Gallery. It takes on a different form. At the National Gallery it is part of the monumental structure. Here it becomes legible as house-like elements that make up the building, but their identity and autonomy as pavilions are maintained. At Peabody it all blends together under the glass roof.

At Stuttgart there was a crane, all the galleries that could be changed by the artists. You can't design every conceivable gallery, so why not let people create these spaces as they need them and replace them, around the frame of the building. It becomes a cultural statement, very dynamic—where other architects could contribute to its changing nature. I think it's a radical idea still worth pursuing and realizing.

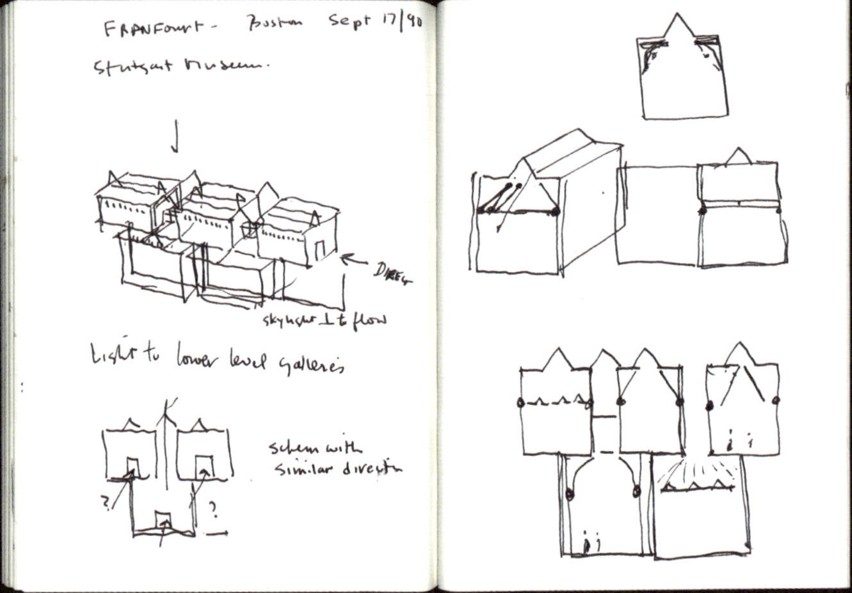
FRANFOURT - Boston Sept 17/90
Stutgart Museum.
DIREC
skylight ⊥ to flow
Light to lower level galleries
schem with
similar directn

2 M

what
is entry
all about??

Model, sectional view, light wells and stacked day-lit galleries, 1990

What about the idea of a building in motion that is constantly changing? Have you explored that in later projects?

I haven't. A little bit in Munich, but we have not gone back to it. It would be a great commission; to explore it with a client who believes in it. It's an idea we should come back to.

Model, 1990

Super-conducting Super Collider

Waxahachie, Texas, USA
1992–1993

The client for this complex to house the world's largest and most advanced machine for high-energy physics research wanted a campus master plan and design guidelines for outbuildings at intervals along the 59-mile accelerator tunnel. The accelerator's cooling pond anchors the campus. The pond's west side contains offices and labs forming the community's private side, which would grow in layers like a mill town along a river. The east side's public facilities include an education center, a hotel, and villas for visiting scientists. Joining public and private across the water is a double-height bridge building with cafeterias, meeting rooms, a large auditorium, a library, and two experiment control rooms. Transparent and open towards the water on the south, rounded and dam-like toward the north, this long link provides the opportunity for interaction among all members of the community.

The US Congress suspended work on the project in 1993.

Model, 1993

The Super Collider is a fascinating project. When I look at other projects that came after—Delmar Hospital, Exploration, the Istanbul master plan, and of course Crystal Bridges—all those "kids" can be seen in this project. Do you see it as a breakthrough?

At several levels, yes. As an institution of research, I was probably thinking of the Salk Institute, where a concentrated number of scientists are working in labs. I was considering a campus of research, with a meeting place, a conference center, all of the amenities. Kahn's original scheme for the Salk, with its meetinghouse and residential villages, was not built. There was a project we did in the 1970s—the Institute for Desert Research in Negev, Israel—that we thought of as a community of researchers and a support network that works with them, that drew from Kahn's approach. At the Super Collider we were designing for thousands of scientists and a major installation of scientific facilities. How do you create a place that induces interactivity? We looked at Fermilab in Illinois—a high-rise structure that wasn't conducive at all to creating community.

Model (44 x 34 x 9 inches H), 1993

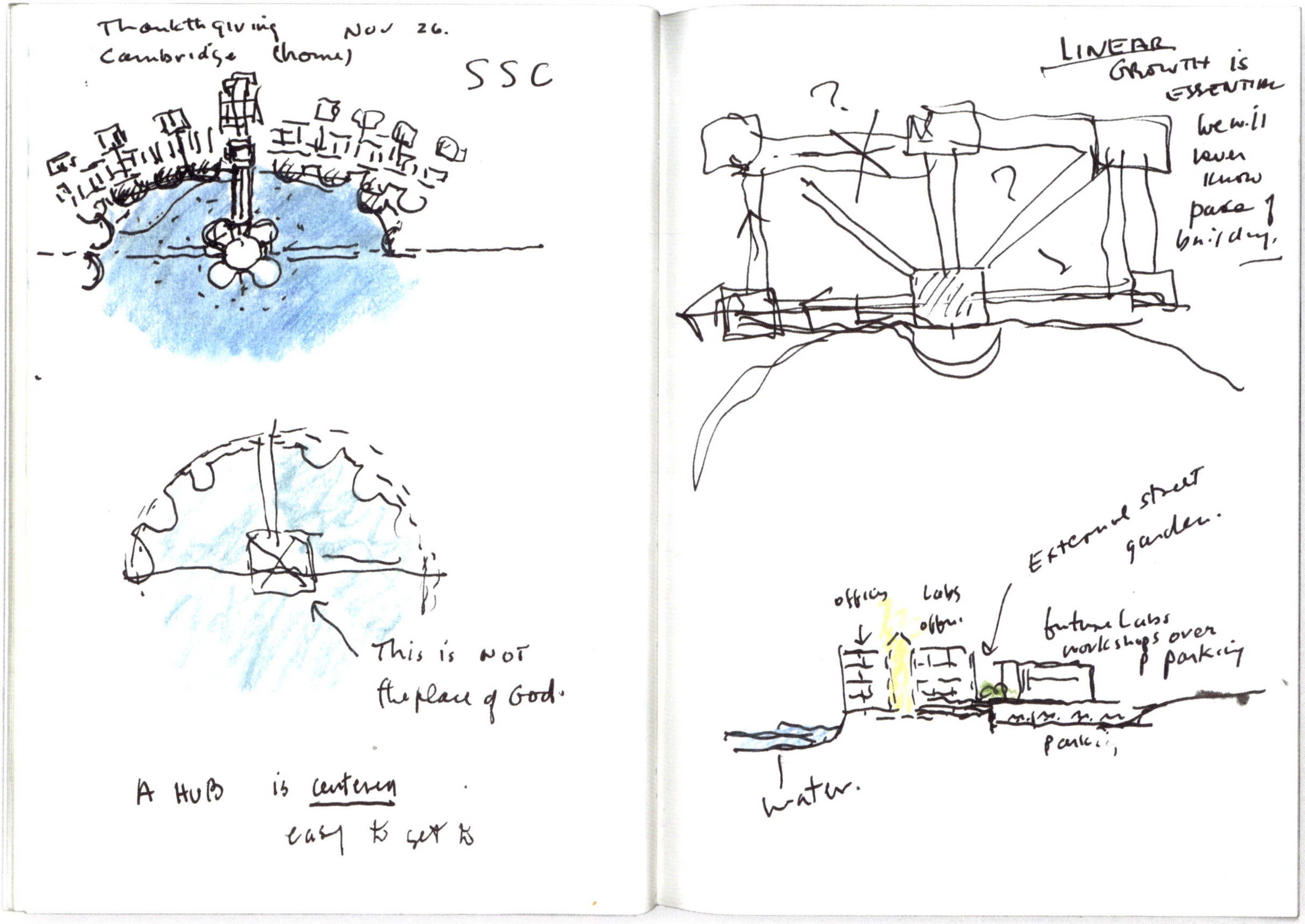

Sketch, ink and pastel, Sketchbook 78
Moshe Safdie, 1992

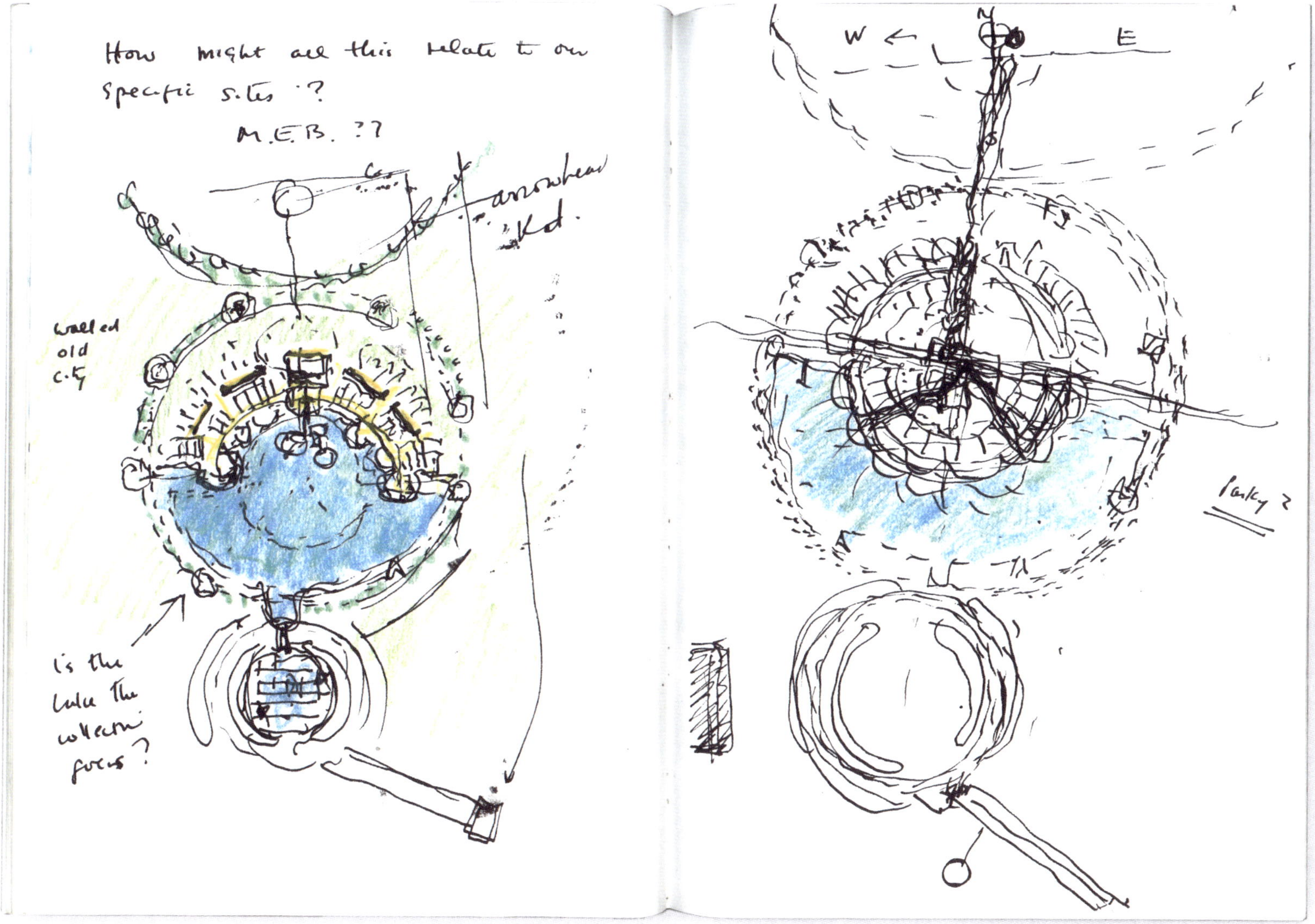
How might all this relate to our specific sites ?
M.E.B. ??
arrowhead Rd.
walled old city
is the lake the collection focus ?
W
N
E

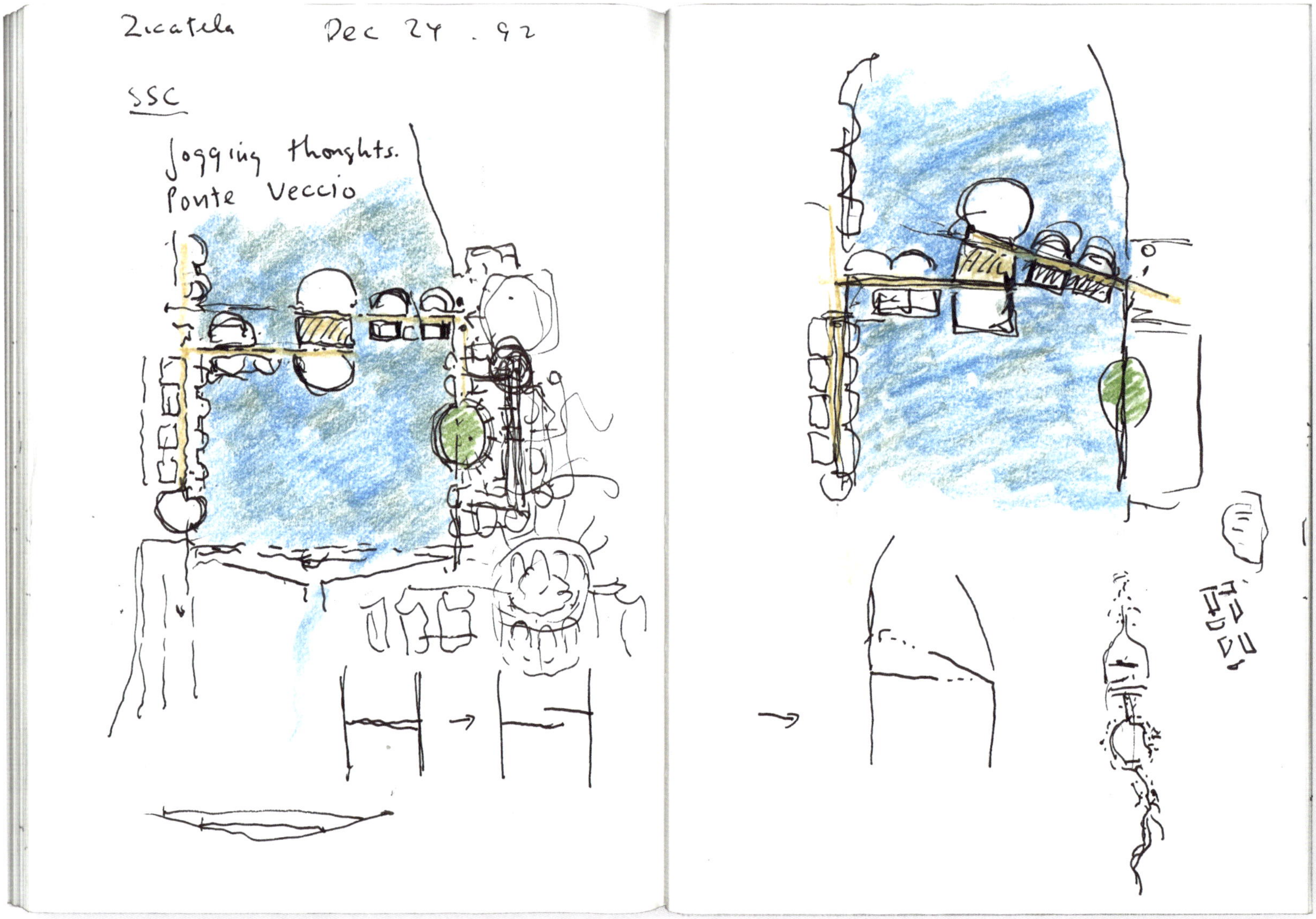

Sketch, ink and pastel, Sketchbook 78
Moshe Safdie, 1992

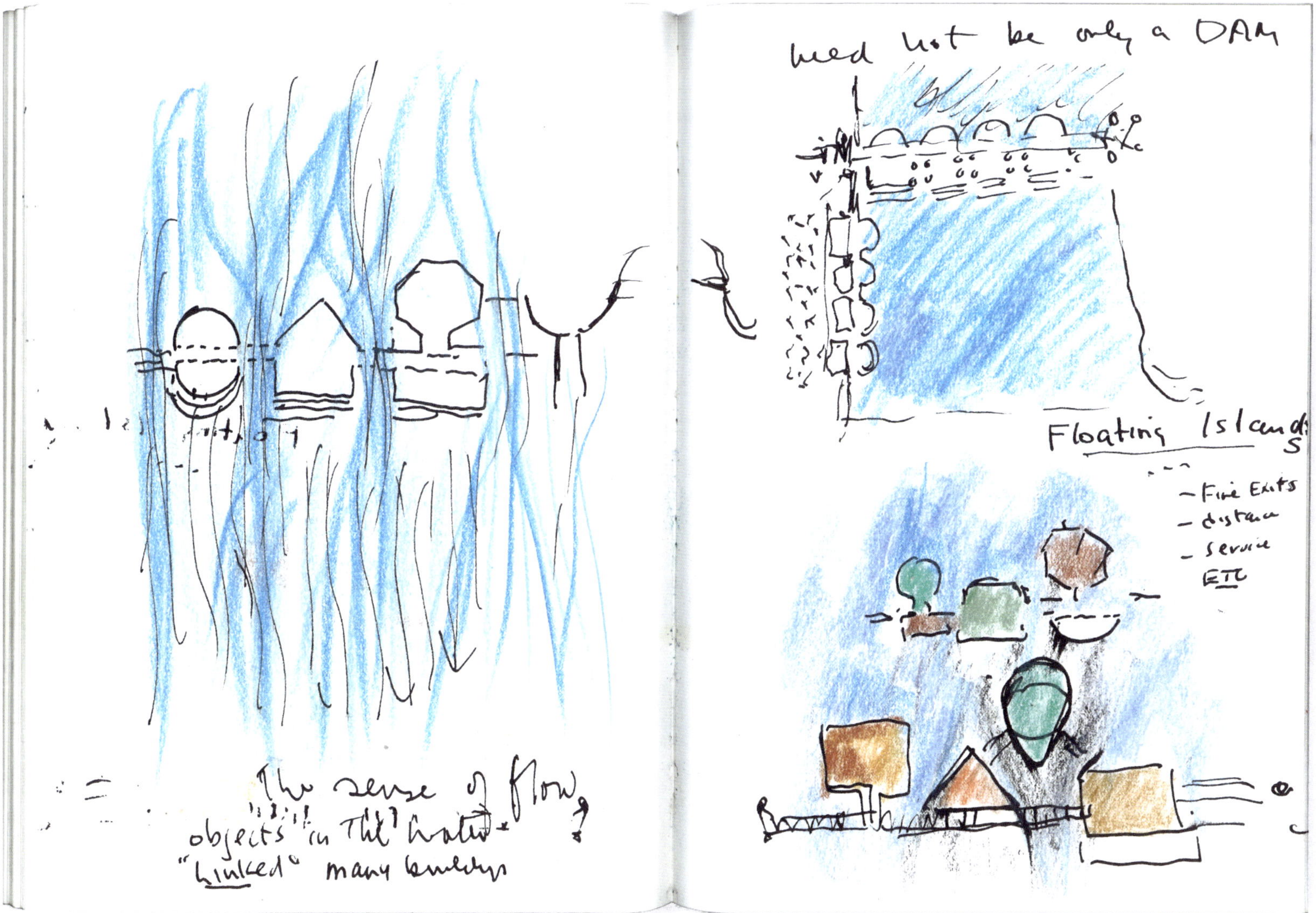
The sense of flow
objects in The water
"Linked" many buildings
need not be only a DAM
Floating Islands
- Fire Exits
- distance
- service
ETC

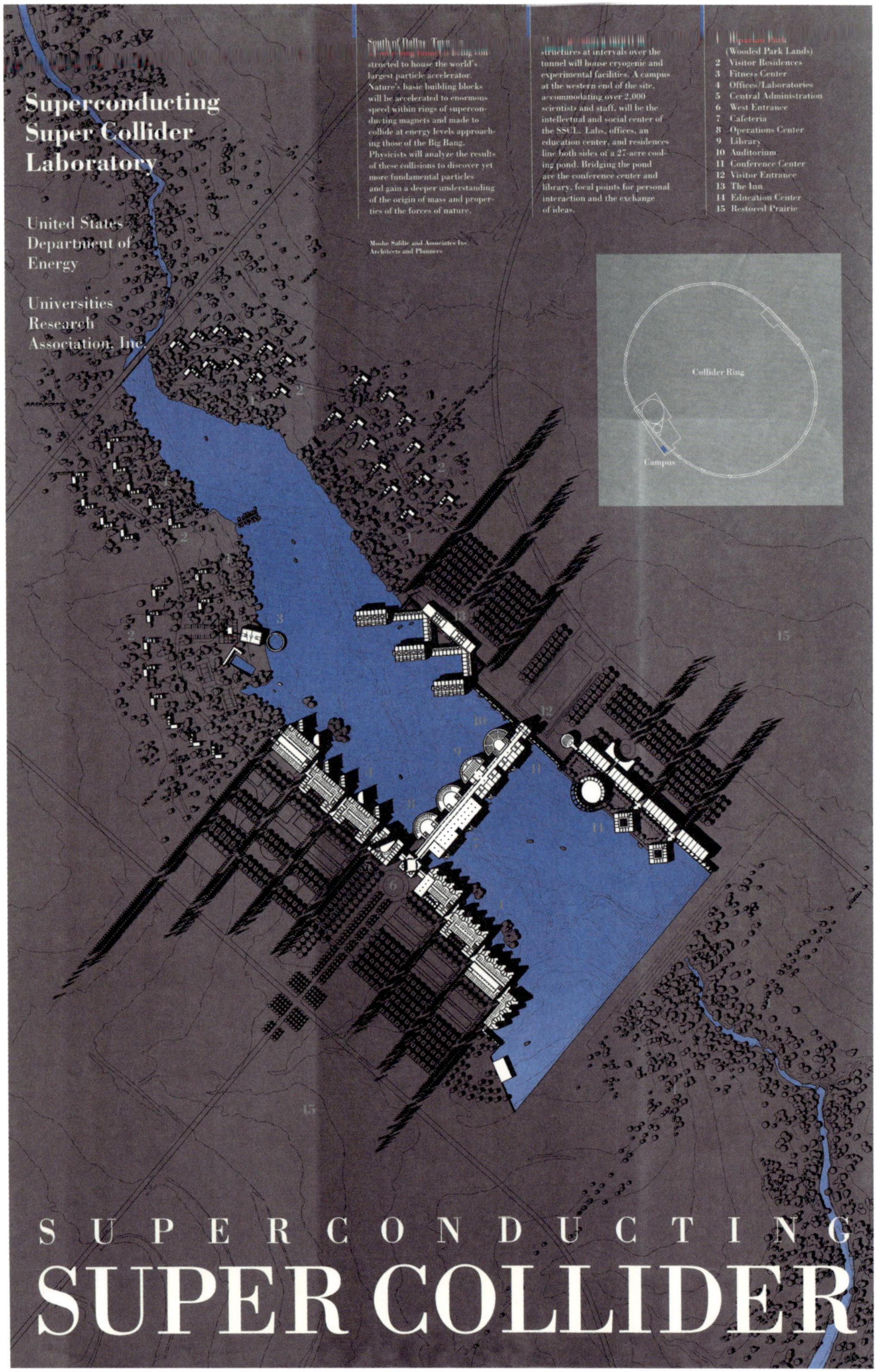

Poster, US Department of Energy and Universities Research Association, 1993

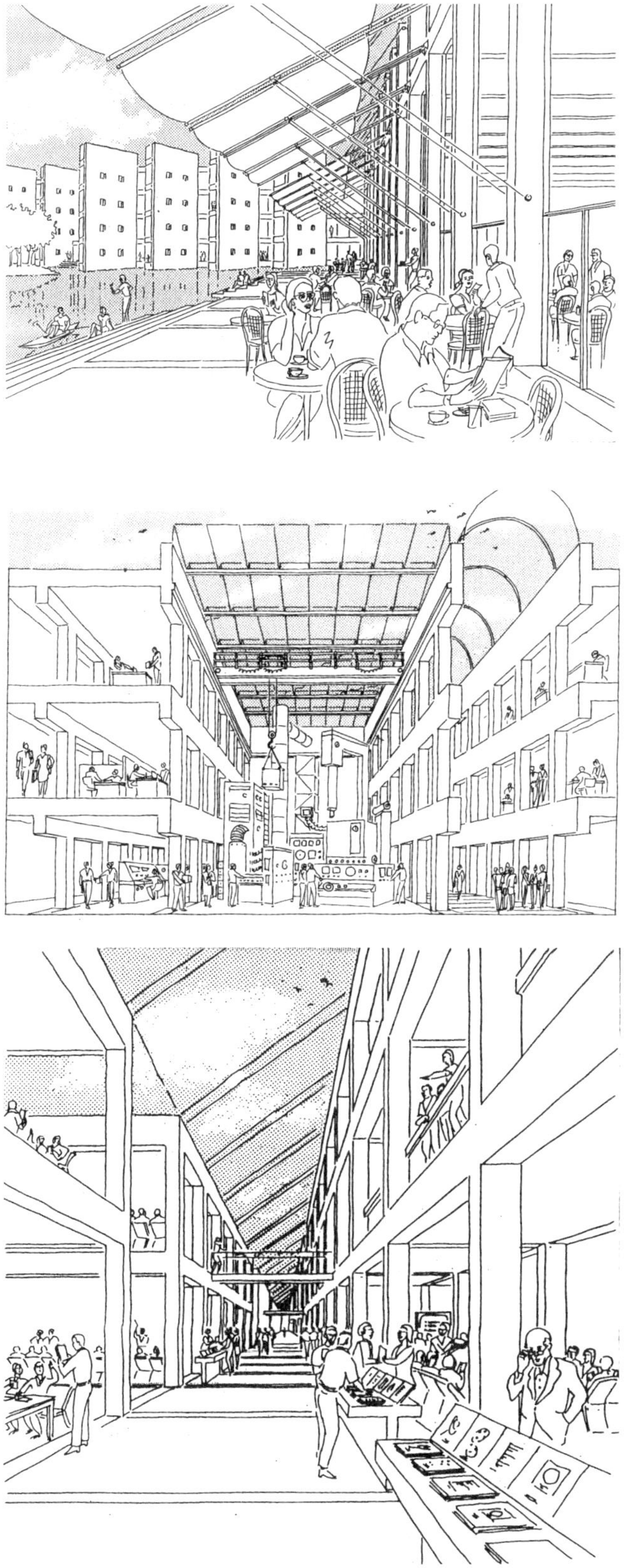

We went to CERN in Switzerland (before the Hadron collider was built)—a rambling collection of low-rise buildings with lots of paths and interactions, a big cafeteria in the middle, and that was much more conducive. We evolved a design with the labs and offices on one side, and the residential hotel and villages for families on the other. The facility was to be so vast that you needed cryogenic pools to cool down the detectors in the 59 miles of collider tunnels. You had to excavate the tunnels, so you had lots of earth to dispose of. We designed a kit of parts for the auxiliary structures, earthworks built with the excavated earth. The cryogenic pond became the centerpiece, with the campus built around a body of water. It gave us a natural lake, which people crossed to go from the labs to the residences. On that bridge, that's where we put the library, restaurants, auditorium, conference rooms—where people rub shoulders.

Vignette sketches, ink, interior spaces of campus, 1993

The idea of architecture floating on the water is the overwhelming concept of this design. We see that again and again in your later work. Is that the breakthrough here?

Yes! There's magic when buildings sit in or on water, because of the reflections. The Château de Chenonceau, even the Parliament building on the Thames has that—it's so enriching. I remember being impressed with some of the buildings in St Petersburg sitting directly on water. At Crystal Bridges we created the water by creating two dams, which was exciting. There are other influences—mill towns that employ dams for waterpower. There was a project that preceded the Super Collider—the Beit Clal conference center in northern New York, in 1988. We dammed the pond and bridged it with buildings. This idea gets revisited in Exploration Place, where one of the buildings is an island, and in an unrealized master plan for North Station in Boston, where we built over an island.

Model, plan view, 1993

Palm Jumeirah Gateway Mosque

Dubai, United Arab Emirates
2007–2008

The archipelago of Palm Jumeirah is a triangular site bounded by two bridges. Accommodating 2000 worshippers on the tight site prompted a reinterpretation of traditional mosque spaces—typically a prayer hall abutting an ablution courtyard. The design's courtyard with ablution pool occupies the entire parcel, with the prayer hall hovering above, contained within a 125-foot sphere set on concrete piers. A great ellipsoid cuts the sphere's lower portion; a catenary roof covers the prayer hall. The asymmetrical cut allows the Mecca axis to rise to the sphere's full height, resulting in a crescent moon profile. A necklace of skylights marks the meeting point of roof and sphere, allowing daylight to enter from the mosque's entire perimeter. Enclosing the center of the mosque is a dome clad in gold leaf and penetrated by pins of light—an iconic image on the city's skyline.

Digital rendering
Section perspective, 2008

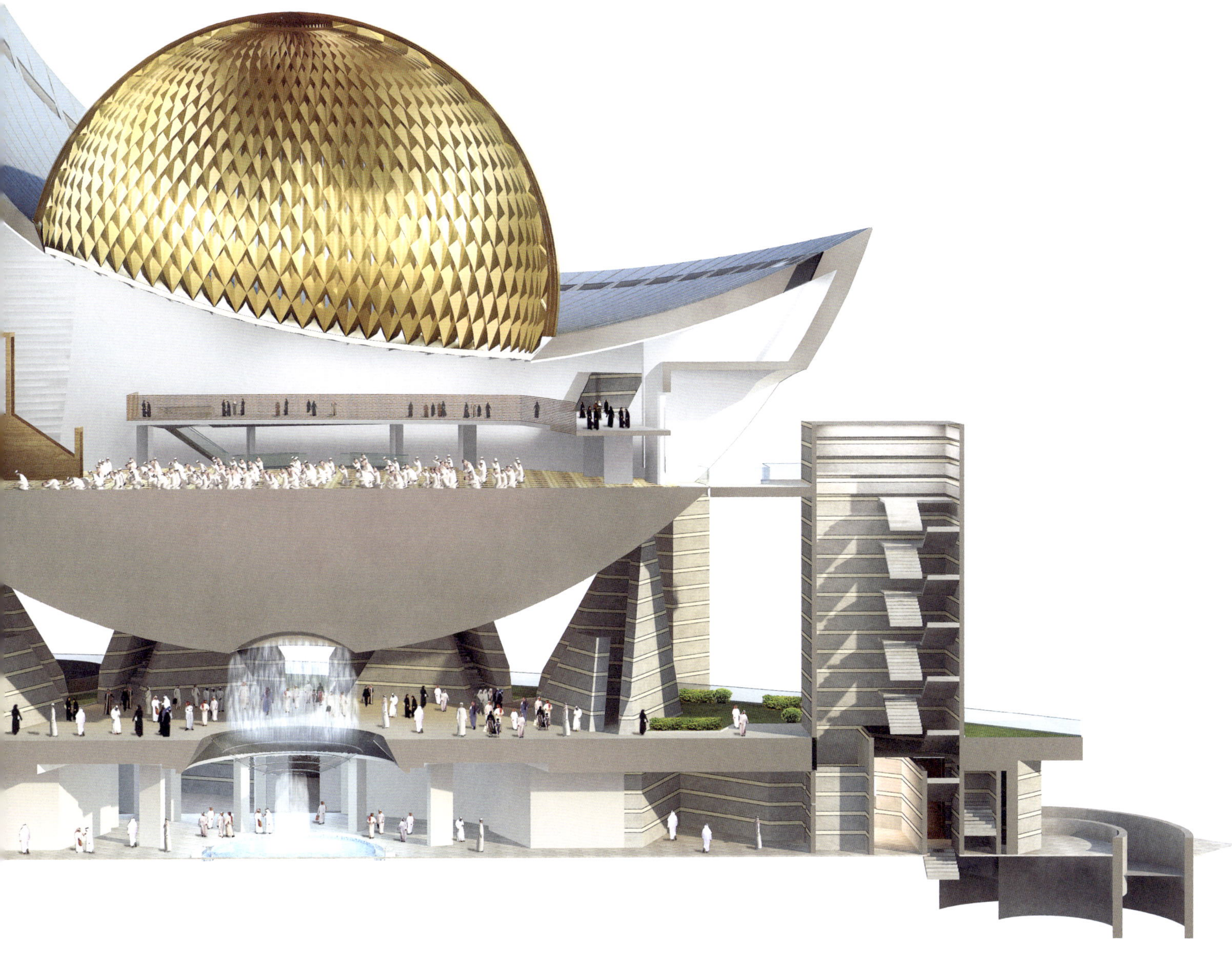

Watercolor rendering, Michael McCann, 2008

The Jumeirah Gateway Mosque seems to take the typically horizontal distribution of mosque spaces and elements—the ablution area, prayer hall, dome, quibla wall—and arranges them vertically. How did this occur; is this idea of inversion an approach you've taken in other projects?

In part it is site driven. The site is a little triangle between three roads. I realize there's a lot of cheek with an Israeli Jew taking on a mosque in Dubai, so I wanted to be sensitive to Islamic traditions. I recruited Oleg Grabar who had been the authority at Harvard on Islamic architecture.

I wanted to understand the differences between the Shia and the Sunni, and what happens in the mosque step by step. Could a minaret be part of the building, not a separate tower? He showed me precedents. Some things I accepted as given; I might have more of a problem in an Orthodox synagogue separating men and women, but that's because I'm critical of Orthodox Jewry for not reforming.
In the mosque I was not going to be a reformer. They were thrilled that it was formally so different, but symbolically right on. It captures the symbolism of the sun

McCANN '08

and moon, the movement of the elements with the moon cycle, the light coming in with the minaret.

Putting the ablution under the building made sense and was ritualistically appropriate. The stacking made ritualistic sense and was logical with the site. I'm just sorry that this was never built because it would have been fascinating to see how it stood the test of use.

Watercolor renderings.
Michael McCann, 2008

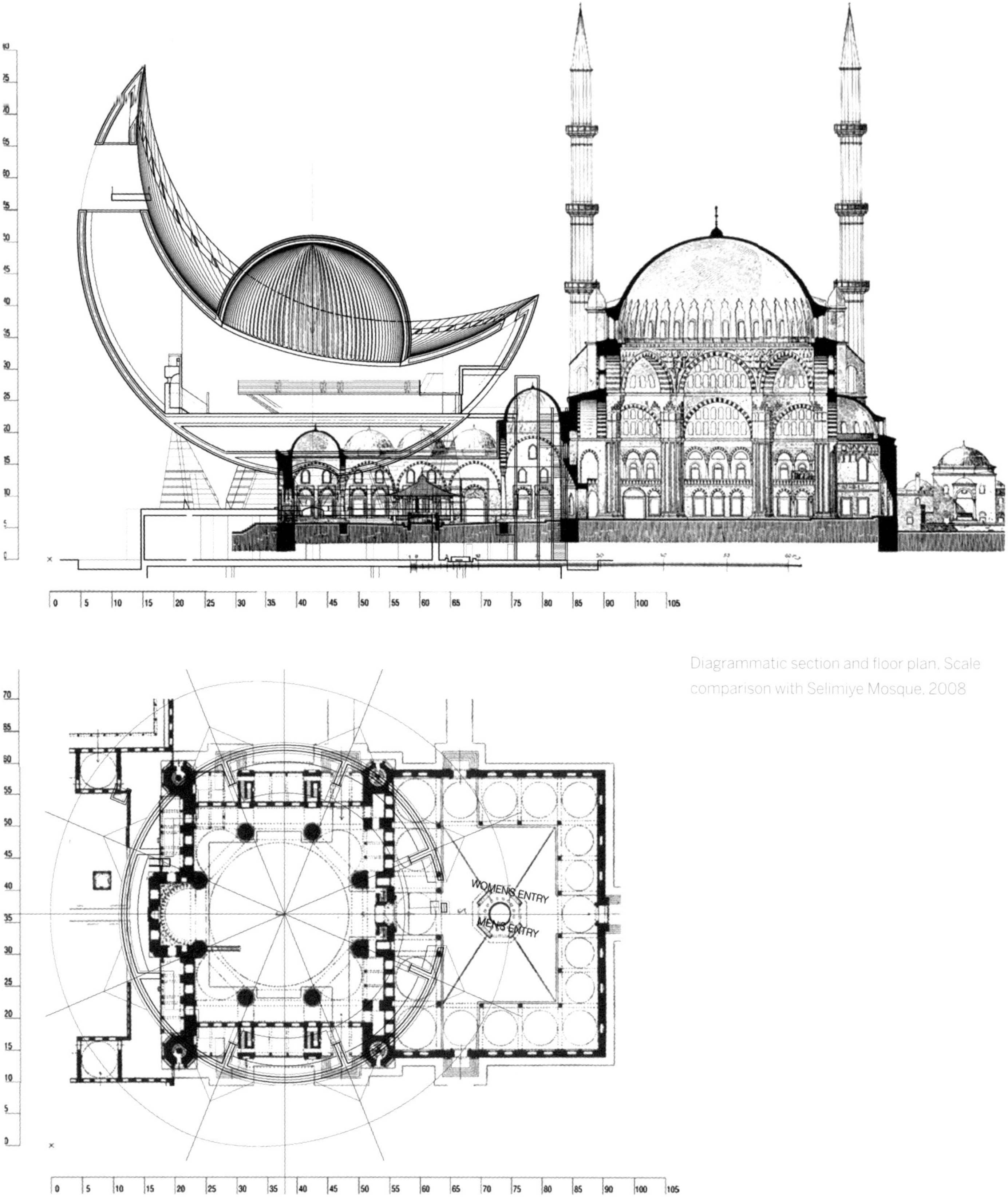

Diagrammatic section and floor plan. Scale comparison with Selimiye Mosque, 2008

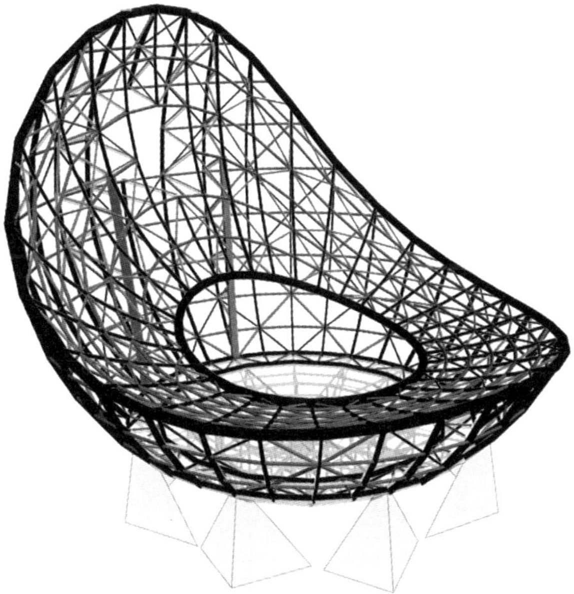

Digital structural model, axonometric, 2008

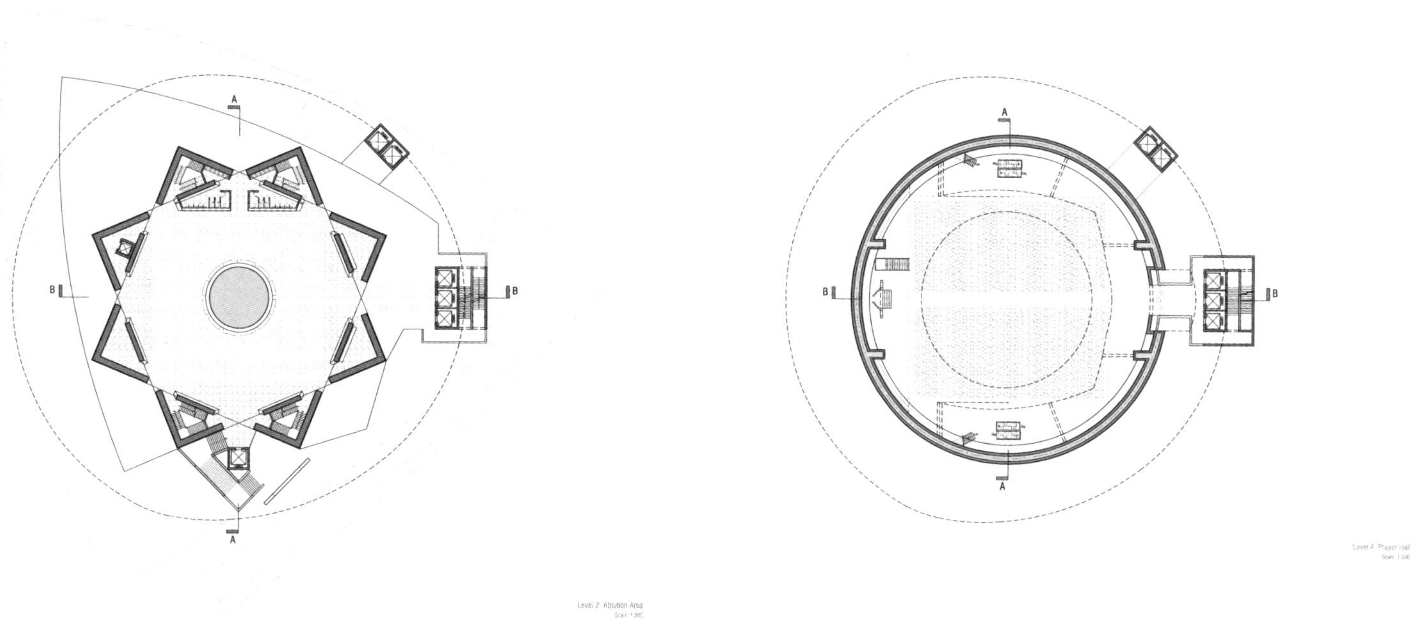

Floor plan drawing, ablution courtyard and prayer hall, 2008

Model (24 x 33 x 18 inches H), 2008

Model (24 x 33 x 18 inches H), 2008

Incheon Int'l Airport Terminal 2

Seoul, Korea
2011

The most significant decision in designing a new airport is the development of an appropriate organizational diagram for the terminal, one that optimizes passenger convenience and operational efficiency. This design's efficient organization concentrates the gates within three pods, served by a main passenger-processing terminal, all connected through a series of welcoming gardens by way of a highly efficient intra-airport rapid transit system. By focusing on inherent aspects of human behavior, the design allows a clearer sense of orientation, increases the speed with which passengers reach the gates, decreases walking distances, and brings passengers closer to nature, amenities, and retail outlets. The goal is to design a more pleasant and comfortable environment—a quintessentially Korean airport. The design echoes Korea's architectural heritage and culture by deploying warm, natural materials, and celebrating nature and the garden tradition.

Digital rendering, 2011

Digital rendering, 2011

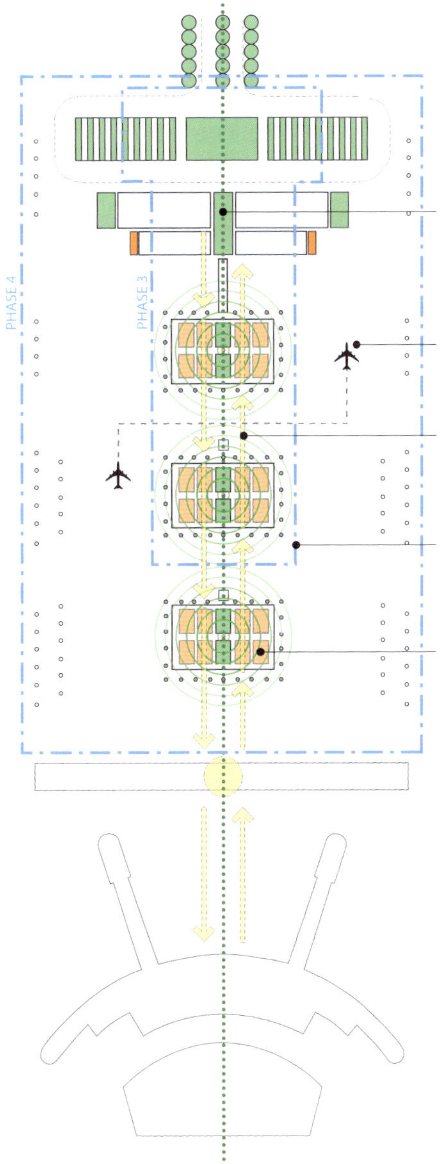

Programmatic diagram (distribution, movement, and phasing), 2011

Incheon Airport is a case where the design challenged the presumptions of the client, in this instance the idea of how to organize the flow through the terminal.

It's worth talking a bit about the program of a building, how architects come to terms with programs. Some people think that the program is the prerogative of the client, because it is what their needs are and you are the interpreter of it. I've discovered that clients are good at defining quantitatively what their needs arc, but not so articulate about qualitative needs. For instance, a program for a school tells you how many classrooms, how many kids in each class, but is silent about the quality of light, the ability to transform the room, the nature or character of gathering space, or even sound levels. So architects supplement quantitative programs with qualitative programs. In airports there is enormous variation in response to program.

You have airports that are enormous structures with long walking distances, you have satellites connected by tunnels or trains. Often we're given a diagram about how the airport is going to work, but it might not be optimal.

Digital rendering, section perspective, 2011

At Incheon they had built multiple, parallel satellite terminals connected by trains—the Denver or Atlanta model. They were not happy with it, so the new terminal was going to the opposite extreme: one building with enormous walking distances. They didn't link effectively to the old terminal and everything was premised on retail, compromising passenger comfort. We decided to challenge it and came forth with a diagram that was not the same linear satellite they'd abandoned, but a variation. Of the three satellites, the first one was physically attached, not even dependent on a train. The first 25 gates were directly accessible. But clearly they were married to their preconception.

We spent a lot of money testing the waters and learned a lot doing it. It's the willingness to question the presumptions of the client. I think that's what makes the difference between an architect who considers himself a sole designer versus a partner with the client in interpreting the program—thinking about it in a new way. The competition process doesn't allow you to dialogue with the client. In regular commissions, I consider that our role. It's in our DNA.

A7
A8
A9

Digital renderings, 2011

At Ben Gurion Airport, and also in Toronto Pearson Airport, we convinced the client to change the diagram to great improvement. The key word here is responsibility—to question the program, you need to know it inside out, you have to immerse yourself and become an expert. It has to do with values—how big should an office floor be, what about the light quality? These are all value-laden questions with economic repercussions.

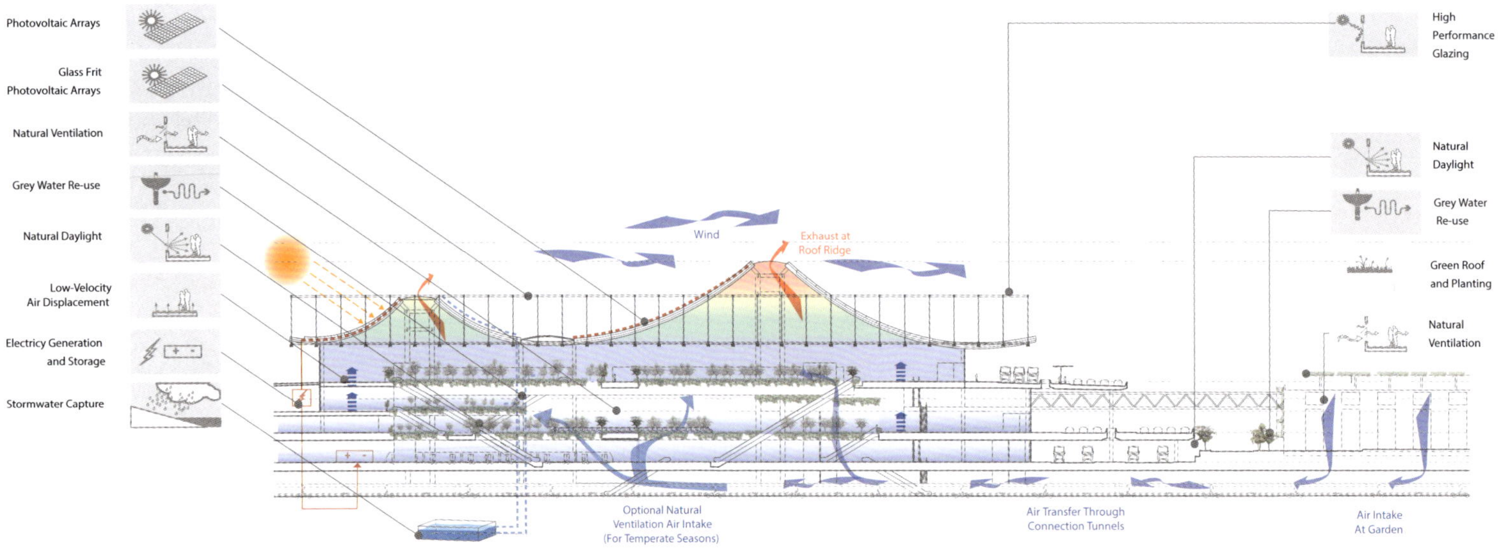

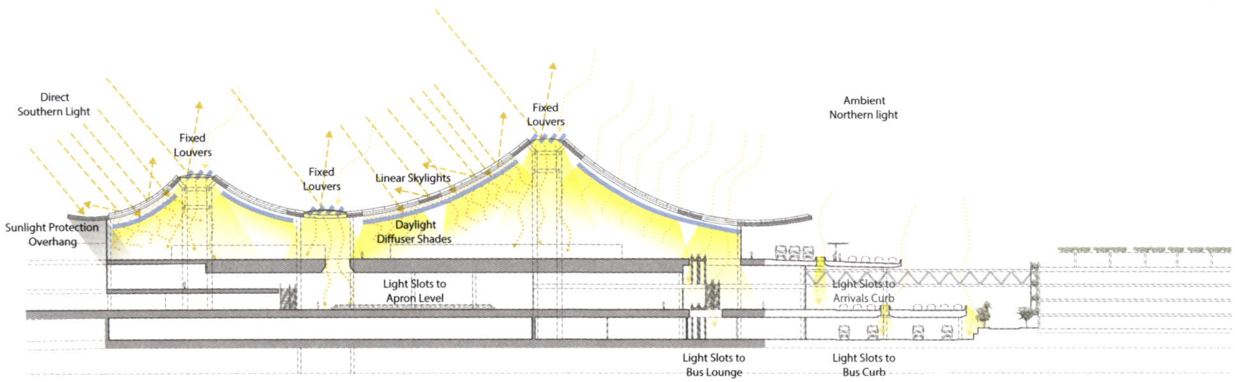

Above: Diagrams, sustainable methods and sunlight, 2011

Opposite: Digital rendering, 2011

National Art Museum of China

Beijing, China
2012

Located along a cultural axis of the city, this competition design is an extroverted expression of the 21st-century museum: transparent, inviting, visible. Housing a series of multistory galleries as a sequence of chambers, the arrangement recalls China's Mogao Caves filled with well-preserved painting and sculpture along the historic Silk Road. The visitor always returns to the western cliff to overlook the city's grand axis, the valley, and views of the lake and surrounding institutions. One circulates into a grand public space of terraces, designed in the tradition of Chinese landscapes and gardens—full of surprising juxtapositions of plants, water, sculpture, and places of intimacy and contemplation. Descending to the west from the ridgetop toward the urban window, the great roof unifies the museum—part of the larger ensemble of public cultural landmarks on the skyline. Both solid and translucent, it supports the building's energy strategy.

Digital rendering, view of west from cultural axis, 2012

Above left: Digital rendering, west façade, 2012

Above right: Photograph, Mogao Caves of Dunhuang, 1982

For the National Art Museum of China, you took a cultural treasure, the Mogao Caves in Dunhuang, China, as inspiration—a living memory for many of the people who would visit it.

When I visited the site for the museum, I was struck by the fact that this grand axis, which begins at the Forbidden City and continues through Beijing, still has meaning. The Olympic Stadium is placed along that axis, and museums are planned to line both sides. In the heart of all of this would be the National Art Museum. There was the axis, but there was a feeling of nothingness, emptiness, it was vacant. I started thinking about a building that celebrates the axis, a building with a front and back, that has a face to the axis and a face to the city. We started thinking that the face to the axis should be very transparent, with galleries stacked one above the other, where the public would circulate on terraces, facing the axis, and enter different galleries. At that point, we decided to engage an expert and scholar on Chinese art and history to inform what we were doing.

We were introduced to Hao Sheng, the Wu Tung Curator of Chinese Art at the Museum of Fine Arts, Boston. He came to the office, looked at a model, and instantly proclaimed, "You have recreated the Mogao Caves of Dunhuang. There it is. Galleries stacked on top of each other with little walkways connecting them—that's Dunhuang." I had never been to Dunhuang. So we looked it up and, lo and behold, there it was. Hao Sheng impressed upon us that the interpretive narrative of a design—a story linked to deep meaning—was fundamental to the Chinese appreciation of architecture. It was their basis of ensuring that a design was not willfully capricious or arbitrary. When we traveled to Beijing to present our design to the director of the museum and the other members of the selection committee, and the slides of Dunhuang flashed as inspiration, their eyes lit up. It did something. It resonated with them, so much so that they recommended that we travel to Dunhuang. We went down the Silk Road, and it was very, very beautiful. It reminded me of the deserts I knew in the Middle East and North Africa.

Collage/model, 2012

ALONG THE SILK ROAD

INSPIRED BY LONGES
LIVING MUSEUM OF CHINA

Sketch, ink and pastel
Sketchbook 167
Moshe Safdie, 2010

We traveled to the escarpment, the cliff where the caves are. The advantage of having come with the head of the National Art Museum was that the 24 caves that are never open to the public were opened to us. We spent two days going from cave to cave and seeing the most incredible Buddhist art and paintings and statues, and taking in the site and its drama, and the river that flows in front of it.

Our design submission got us through the first round of twelve into the short shortlist of the four that were to go forward to another stage of development. This trip occurred between the two. The scheme evolved dramatically. It became sharper and more focused—very much because of that trip to Dunhuang. We made it even more so like Dunhuang. You can see the austere walls with large openings, people walking on the narrow cliffs, with a plateau above, that evolved into a lush garden—an oasis with sculpture, light, and greenery. A giant suspension roof, evoking the roof architecture of the Forbidden City and of the great temples and palaces, hangs over the terraces below. It is suspended on a catenary structure, anchored on either side by two volumes—the entry pavilion and the great hall.

Digital rendering, terraces and gardens, 2012

This was a whole year of design effort with a lot of dialogue. In parallel, Zaha Hadid, Jean Nouvel, and Frank Gehry were laboring away. Nouvel won. We were disappointed. These are the ones that are painful to lose.

The design echoes other projects you were doing at the time—like the bold, sculptural geometric solids of the Kauffman Center for the Performing Arts, and perhaps the ArtScience Museum in Singapore.

It is certainly reminiscent of Kauffman, which has a glass roof soaring above the atrium that serves as the foyers for both of the halls. Kauffman encouraged us that it was possible to achieve this at a grander scale.

Digital rendering, east façade, 2012

This book's subtitle includes the term "unrealized dreams." The story about Hao Sheng discovering the caves in the initial design, it strikes me as a dream you might have had about Dunhuang. You didn't remember the dream, but somehow it found its way into the design.

There is something about this scheme. It is a landscape. It's almost the essence of China. Of all the projects we've lost, I couldn't understand this one. I thought that deploying very advanced, cutting-edge engineering to achieve some very traditional themes was a nice counterpoint, showing that China can build the most complex, technologically demanding building, and it's doing so in the spirit of its traditions in architecture.

Digital rendering, interior sculpture garden, 2012

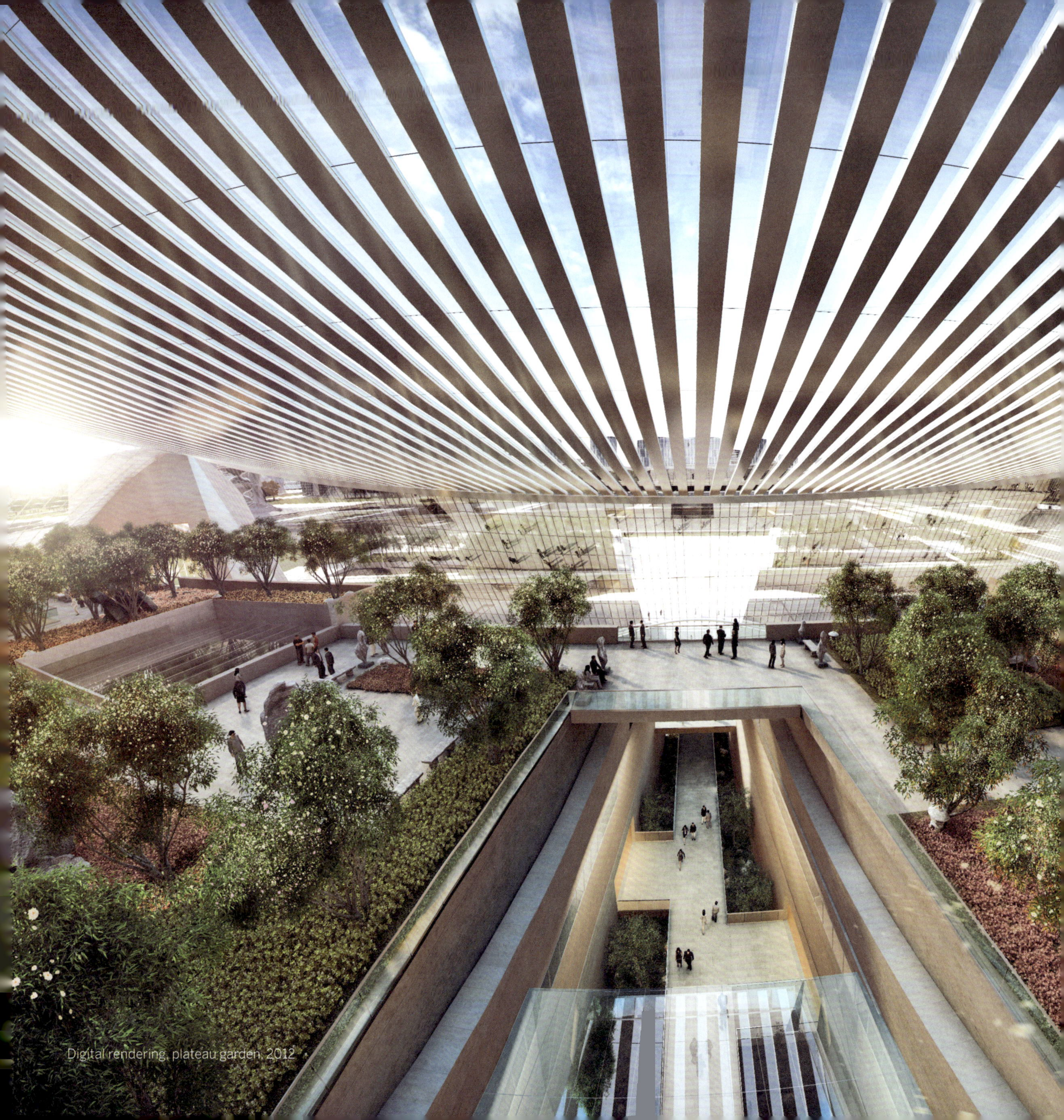

Digital rendering, plateau garden, 2012

Above: Digital rendering, gallery chamber, 2012

The Abrahamic Family House

Abu Dhabi, United Arab Emirates
2019

The Abrahamic Family House in Abu Dhabi is a landmark project showcasing the role tolerance and inclusion plays in UAE culture and heritage. The project brings together a mosque, synagogue, and church within a shared public park set in the cultural district of Saadiyat Island. With an underlying concept of Diversity Within Unity, the design envisions each of the three worship halls as a variation of the sphere. Considered a sacred form, the sphere symbolizes oneness, and the equity before God of all who worship. Its variants, the dome and the circle, are recurring symbols in the sacred buildings of all Abrahamic religions. Set in a body of water, it creates an oasis within the desert environment where water is the embodiment of life. The design of each religion's unique and specific worship space evokes the history, traditions, and rituals of the particular religion. Seen together, they form an integrated and unified whole.

Digital rendering, aerial view, 2019

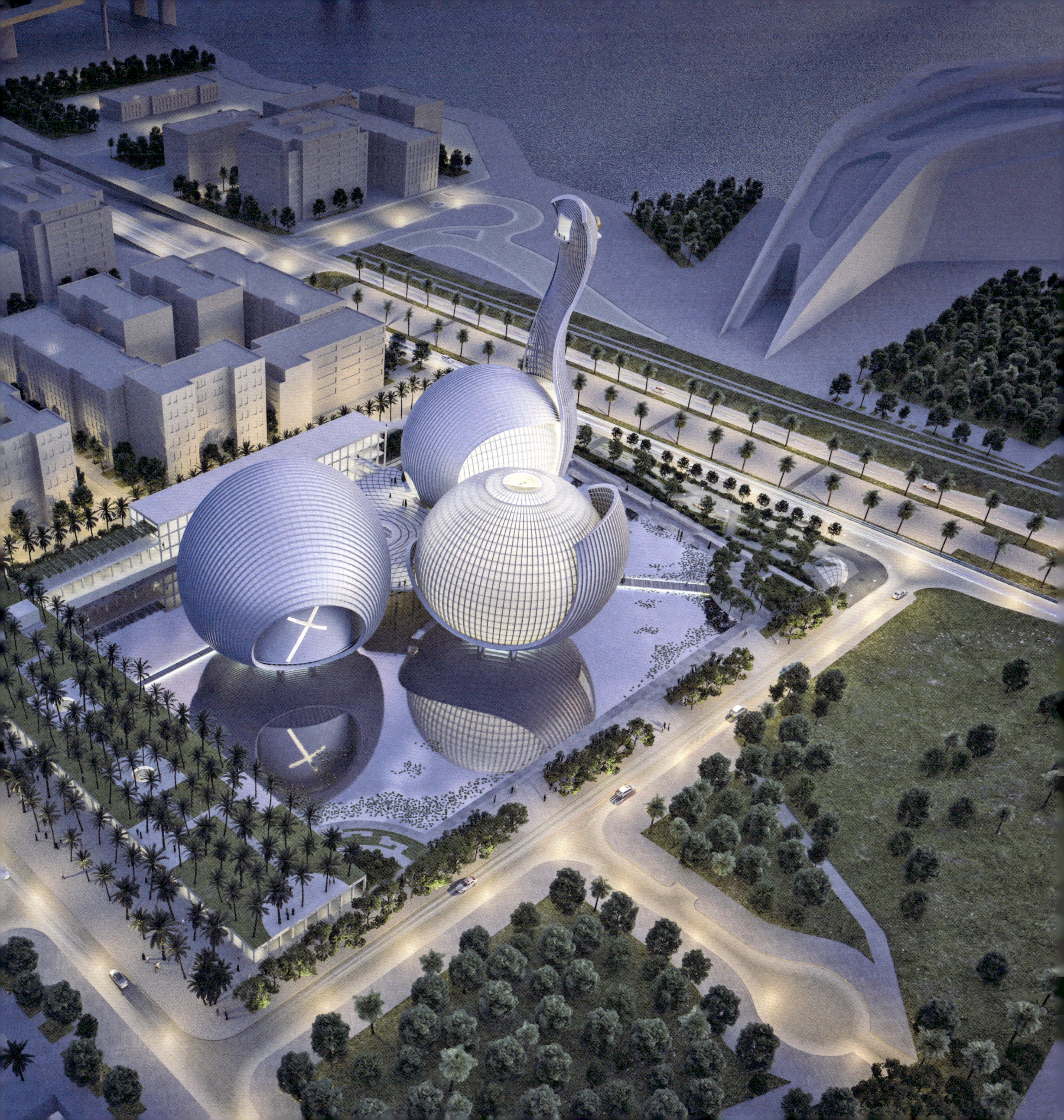

Digital rendering, aerial view, 2019

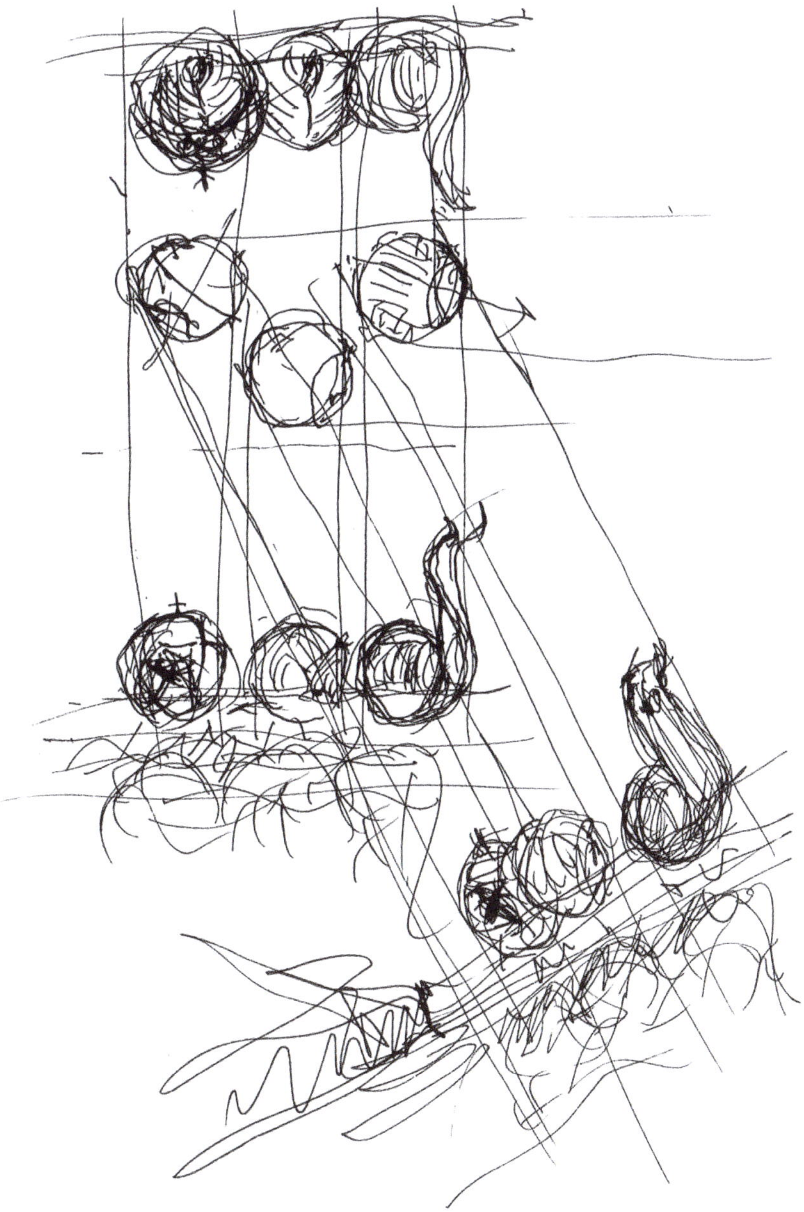

Sketch, ink, Moshe Safdie, 2019

This project appears to be premised on the interplay of three elements often seen in your work: geometry, light, and water. How is each expressed in ways that connect to past projects—built and unbuilt, secular and well as religious architecture—that you've designed?

The site, though on Saadiyat Island, is a landlocked parcel. Early on in the design I felt that it might be interesting for the site to become a body of water, like a pond. Initially the forms of the three religious buildings were quite different:
the mosque was derived from the design we proposed for a site in Dubai several years ago, which was not built; the synagogue was somewhat in the spirit of an early synagogue as a cube; the church was a cylinder; the museum was a segmented sphere. When I presented this scheme to the client the reaction was quite negative. They recognized the similarity of the mosque to the one designed for Dubai (as that project was one of the reasons they invited us) and expected something less derivative, given the uniqueness to this program.

Digital rendering, exterior elevation, 2019

I was shocked by their reception, but in a good way. We had four weeks left to conceive of and develop a new design. We went in a completely different direction. The commonality between the three faiths is strong—the role of Abraham, the Bible, the Prophets. That led to the sphere as the common element. It's obviously difficult, and tenuous, to balance a sphere on a foundation, so the body of water mediates that. The water dematerializes the ground plane. With their reflections in the water, these objects visually become complete spheres, able to be viewed in full form. To do that, we raised the level of the worship halls 33 feet above the street. You enter into the complex in an arrival plaza and are contained by the three spheres, in the space found between them.

What is the role of light—a strong element in much of your architecture—in this design?

There are two kinds of light. In this Middle East setting light often comes filtered through the fine grill of the mashrabiya or the Indian jali. There is also clear light that comes through skylights. In all three religious structures there are opaque,

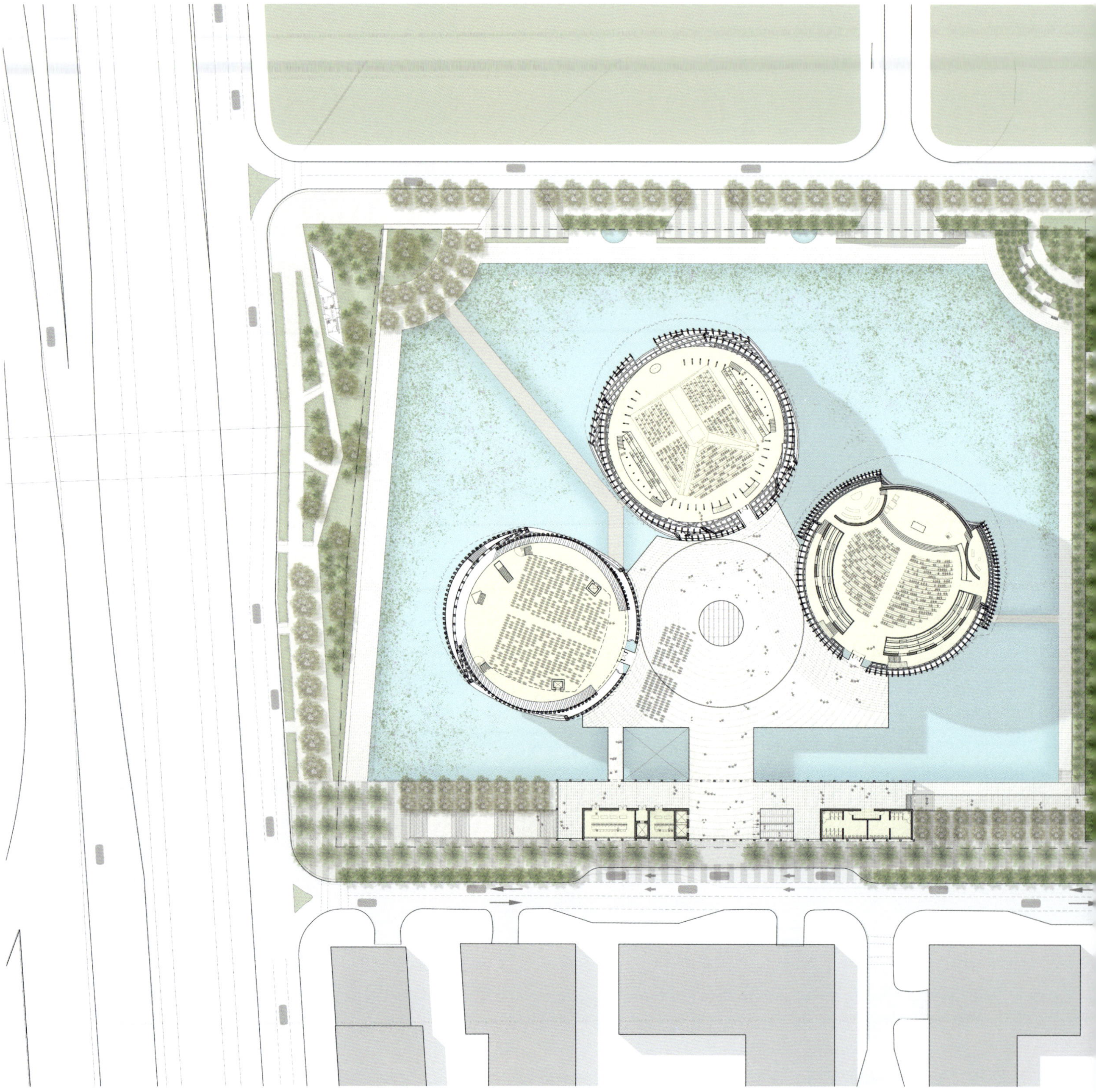

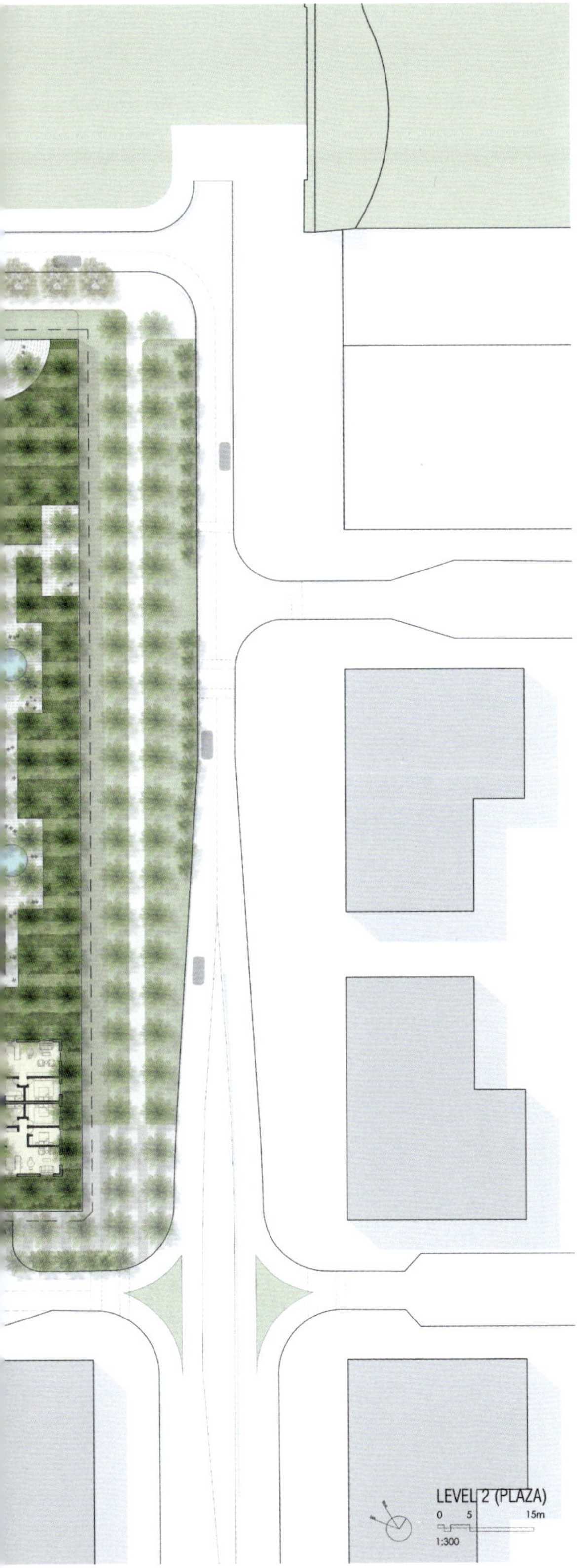

translucent, and lattice walls with clear glass, and these layers sometimes overlap each other. The sphere of the mosque forms a minaret, reaching for the sky. The synagogue is the most understated in its expression. The richness of it is seen in the interior, which reflects the Sephardic tradition of sitting in the round; reinforced with a toroidal-shaped screen within the sphere. The church has a series of walls inside the main volume. The cross is from a church we designed to be built in Cartagena, Columbia—the inclined cross symbolizing the suffering of Christ as he carried it. You see it from the exterior. I think each faith is expressed clearly as what it is, but the commonality is in the geometry and the treatment of light.

How did your choice of materials in this project contribute to the sense of the sacred that you wished to convey in this design?

I wanted something that had the quality of the mashrabiya, but at a much larger scale, with significant spans. We knew from our experience designing and building Jewel Changi Airport that it

Site plan drawing, Level 2 – Plaza, 2019

Digital rendering, interior church, 2019

would have to be steel. It would need to be fabricated out of welded steel lattice in two directions. This is a very efficient structure because it takes advantage of the spherical geometry and the rigidity of the curved form while maintaining porosity.

This is a recent design. How does it reflect some of your own personal beliefs about the sense of the sacred in architecture?

What I discovered through much of the work is that there is an element of the sacred. I'm not a believer in the traditional sense, an observant Jew, but I believe I'm a highly ethical and spiritual person. What a Jew or a Christian might believe are not strange to me. How can I respond to the emotional charge of a believer? Corbusier did that in Ronchamp. You cannot live in this universe without being filled with awe and wonder at the sublime order of nature. It's clear when you experience this moment of uplift, the space you are in can transport you—when you enter Chartres Cathedral, or the Friday Mosque in Isfahan. I have yet to experience a synagogue that does this in the same way.

Digital rendering, exterior mosque, 2019

Digital rendering, interior mosque, 2019

Digital rendering, interior synagogue, 2019

Sadly, many of the great ones in history are no longer with us. Sacred spirituality is common to all human beings.

For me, this is not confined to religious buildings in my work. I recall walking into the great hall of the National Gallery of Canada in Ottawa, and a little boy was standing there with his mother, looking around, and he said to her: "Does God live up there?" At the Yad Vashem Holocaust History Museum in Jerusalem, there are moments when you are with the sacred. But I also see these qualities in buildings such as Crystal Bridges, and in the Khalsa Heritage Centre. It is something to strive for in all buildings, not only religious ones. Jewel Changi Airport is a commercial venture, but when people are standing around that waterfall, there is something sacred about this space. When the sun hits the waterfall, it's like a revelation.

We lost this competition, but I believe that what we explored here will see light one day, because it is too good not to be built.

Model, 2019

The Lessons of Unbuilt Architecture

Sketch, ink and pastel,
Sketchbook 57, Ballet Opera House
Moshe Safdie, 1989

Unbuilt work presents the architect with a "teaching moment": What can be learned from an unrealized design? There are several possibilities. It could be the level of detail in a design not realized, the interaction with clients and those who have real power to make a project happen, understanding project circumstances that can sink it and avoiding those pitfalls. What have you learned from your unbuilt work over the course of a more-than-50-year practice?

In many competitions you don't have a relationship with the client, and some unbuilt projects are not competitions. The value of a competition is that you focus on an idea very intensely with relatively few distractions, often with fewer inhibitions. The greatest lessons of competitions are the ideas that prevail, that find their way into other projects because of the intensity of the process. It's like a pressure cooker, and sometimes what's left in the pot is enlightening beyond the competition, even if the project's not realized. You might learn how to structure a tall building, or something completely different. It depends on what the project is about and your focus. Considering the projects we've talked about, the lessons are so different depending on the project—what you take from them into your other work.

Do you prefer the competition experience over a commission, generally, with unbuilt work?

It's very different. If a competition design isn't built, it's something you spent two or three months on and that's it—you haven't spent years and gotten attached. When a commission doesn't go forward—a project you've worked hard on—it's far more painful. The problems you've solved are not just conceptual. You've gone through public hearings, permits, code interpretations, meetings—all the things to get a design ready for construction.

With a competition, there is less commitment. It's like you went on a date.

Right—a couple of dates and it didn't work out. With a commission, you get married. But in both cases, potentially there is a lot that gets translated into other work.

What do unbuilt projects teach you about seeing a project to its realization? Would you have done things differently in certain projects not built? Do you ever play the game, "if only..."?

"If only I'd done this" is a game you can play with a built project, too, maybe more so. I'm not big on that. I just go on. I'm not a tormented designer. Once I've built it...sometimes I'm disappointed, but not often.

Might you ask: "Did I do something in a competition that was never won or never built that caused it to be unrealized?"

It rarely happens. Sometimes you do a competition and you see that the winner had a better idea. That can be humbling. Even if it is equally as good it can be food for thought. On an unbuilt project that is not a competition, you might think, "If I'd only addressed a particular issue that I didn't, maybe the outcome would have been different." There was some soul-searching when we lost Singapore airport: "What did we do in our proposal that they found threatening, or was it something done out of stubbornness?" You go through what might have affected a decision.

Ideas carried from one project to another—is that a conscious process?

It's more like residual value. In the National Gallery we invented something new—how to bring light into the lower level. It's an idea, and you don't throw it away. You realize it there, and in a project like the Peabody Museum you use the idea again to bring light in. But it takes on a different life. You might ask, "What if I actually make the shaft legible from the outside?" It's the variation on a theme, on the idea of bringing light in, which prevails. There is always an inventory of ideas that you tried and tested, and use again. That's where a client gets the advantage of accumulated experience.

How do unbuilt projects live on in future work?

Ideas tend to manifest themselves again if they are strong. They can have a continuing impact. What's interesting about that question is the new technology we have. A few years ago, an architect took information available on the most significant of Louis Kahn's unbuilt buildings and produced a series of photorealistic renderings. Because Kahn wasn't one to detail everything—decisions were often made on the site—there was a lot of room for interpretation. Nevertheless, the building came into a new life. Recently we've taken some of our early, unbuilt projects—Pompidou Centre, the Supreme Court of Israel, SFSC Student Union—and created renderings and animations. The original architect still being around to interpret—unlike the case of Kahn—brings the building to life more vividly. They are still just representations, but they have a certain power and have afforded us an understanding of the spaces differently than we had, which reopens the exploration.

The great Chicago architect Daniel Burnham had a quote about unbuilt architecture: "A noble, logical diagram once recorded will never die, but long after we are gone will be a living thing, asserting itself with ever-growing insistency."

That's a beautiful quote. The word "diagram" is used in such a profound way. It's poetic. It's a revelation actually.

How are your unbuilt projects "living things" for you? How do you experience them asserting themselves, across the arc of your work as an architect?

The word diagram, in the sense that Burnham is using it, captures the ability to summarize the essence of a design in a very compact way. Many architects have searched for the right terms to express this. Le Corbusier says the plan is the generator: in the plan you discover the essence of the design, which generates the whole building. For me, the site is the generator because the site possesses in it a diagram as well—there's an essence to each place that I am searching for, trying to express. But for Burnham, the diagram is the sum total of all of that, it's the sum total of the organization of the building, of its relationship to the site, of its relationship to human beings—it is purpose and intent at the same time. A design that has deep meaning and has enough (if I may use a bold word) truth in it, will have a diagram that resonates and lives, because that truth just bursts out, it emerges.

Without being immodest, I think the reason that people respond so strongly to Habitat is that they see in its diagram something that is well beyond itself—this notion that structure can be fractalized and broken up to become almost akin to nature. That's the diagram of it. It goes beyond the individual building. That's what Burnham is saying: the essence of a design has application well beyond its one particular adaptation.

When we're lucky, as architects, and we have insight and maybe modesty, we come upon these diagrams from time to time. Sometimes we borrow those diagrams. I'll give you an example. I was in Louis Kahn's office when he worked on the Salk Institute. There was version one, and version two, which got built. Both had the notion that there was the study where the scientist thinks, and the lab where the scientist physically does things, and the meetinghouse where people congregate to discuss. When I worked on the design of the Superconducting Super Collider, the Salk diagram not only haunted me, it possessed me. While the resultant designs are very different—largely driven in both cases by the uniqueness of each site—the Salk diagram was very helpful. Burnham is telling us, there are all kinds of superfluous things in a design, but there's an essence, a DNA. The diagram is the DNA, and it lives on.

How have the unbuilt projects informed and shaped the core design principles and values—such as creating the public realm, fitness to purpose, buildability, making community, responding to the essence of place, working with nature, humanizing the megascale, and symbolic power—of your own practice?

When you look at the body of the unbuilt work, with few exceptions it is some of the most significant work we've done. Some of it is radical and adventurous, pushing out of the frame or box. The original Habitat proposal pushed much further than the scheme that was built. It pushed beyond the limits of real estate and construction.

Our unbuilt work is where we have been stretching the furthest from convention and the norms. It's a dangerous game, as this stretching of limits might be the factor of not getting built. All have lessons for the long term. Is that true of the unbuilt work of many architects? Probably for an architect like Frank Lloyd Wright, who designed fantastical stuff. It took making this book for me to reflect on this.

What I've concluded is that the unbuilt work is the place you grow the most, and you need to do that. That's how architecture evolves.

Credits & Acknowledgments

Sketch, ink and pastel
Sketchbook 57, Ballet Opera House
Moshe Safdie, 1989

Credits

Cover & page 4

Original sketches by Moshe Safdie

The Nature of Unbuilt Architecture

Original sketch by Moshe Safdie (6)

Public Domain (8, 9, 10)

Estate of R. Buckminster Fuller (11)

Louis I. Kahn Collection, The University of Pennsylvania and the Pennsylvania Historical and Museum Collection (12)

The Unbuilt Projects

Original sketch by Moshe Safdie (14)

Habitat Original Proposal

1964

Architect: Moshe Safdie, Architect

Structural Engineers: Dr. A. Komendant

Client: Canadian Corporation for the 1967 World Exhibition

Image credits:

Original sketch by Moshe Safdie (16–17, 18)

Moshe Safdie (19)

Arnott Rogers (20–21, 22–23, 24)

San Francisco State College Student Union

1967–1968

Architects: Moshe Safdie & Associates with Burger & Coplans Associated Architects

Structural Engineers: Conrad Engineers

Mechanical and Electrical Engineers: Huza Thibault with Hanson & Peterson

Client: College Union Council, San Francisco State College

Image credits:

Carlos Diniz (26–27)

Moshe Safdie (28–29)

The Daily Gater, March 28, 1968 (34 top)

The Daily Gater, October 14, 1968 (34 bottom)

Revolution, March 15, 1969 (35)

Habitat II New York

1967–1968

Architect: Moshe Safdie & Associates

Structural Engineers: Conrad Engineers and T.Y. Lin & Associates

Client: Carol Haussamen Foundation, New York

Image credits:

Original sketch by Moshe Safdie (39 top, 39 middle)

John Halpern (42)

Mike Lawrie (43)

Pompidou Centre

1971

Architect: Moshe Safdie and project team (Heather Willson Cass, Roberta Lawrence, Martin Hoffmeister, Deborah Lee, Clinton Sheerr, James Strickland, Robert Yudell, Henry Wollman)

Client: Ministry of Culture, Government of France

Western Wall Precinct

1971–1994

Architect: Moshe Safdie & Associates

Client: The Company for Reconstruction and Development of the Jewish Quarter and the Municipality of Jerusalem

Image credits:

David Harris (54–55)

Supreme Court of Israel

1985–1986

Architect: Moshe Safdie & Associates

Client: Yad Hanadiv

Image credits:

Original sketch by Moshe Safdie (62–63, 66–67, 70)

Michal Ronnen Safdie (68, 69)

Michael Guran (72, 73)

Columbus Center

1985–1987

Architect: Moshe Safdie & Associates with Emery Roth and Sons, P.C.

Client: Boston Properties and Salomon Brothers Inc.

Moshe Safdie, "Architect's Response," *New York Times,* national edition, November 8, 1987 (85)

Moshe Safdie, "Skyscrapers Shouldn't Look Down on Humanity," *New York Times,* national edition, May 29, 1988 (86–87)

Image credits:

Original sketch by Moshe Safdie (76)

Steve Rosenthal (74–75, 77, 78–79, 83)

Steve Oles (81)

Ada Louise Huxtable, "In the Shadow of the Architect," *Blueprint,* November 1986 (84 top)

James Stevenson, *The New Yorker,* November 23, 1987 (84 bottom)

Ballet Opera House

1987–1990

Architect: Moshe Safdie & Associates and Bregman + Hamann

Acoustical Consultant: Artec Consultants Inc.

Client: Ballet Opera House Corporation

Image credits:

Original sketch by Moshe Safdie (90–91, 92, 94 bottom)

Steve Rosenthal (88–89, 93, 95, 96, 99)

Michal Ronnen Safdie (97)

Museum of Contemporary Art Stuttgart

1990

Architect: Moshe Safdie & Associates

Client: State of Baden-Württemberg, Germany

Image credits:

Original sketch by Moshe Safdie (102, 106)

Michal Ronnen Safdie (100–101, 104, 107, 108–109)

Superconducting Super Collider

1992–1993

Architect: Moshe Safdie & Associates

Client: US Department of Energy and University Research Associates

Image credits:

Original sketch by Moshe Safdie (114, 115, 116, 117)

Michal Ronnen Safdie (110–111, 112–113, 120–121)

US Department of Energy and Universities Research Associates (118)

Palm Jumeirah Gateway Mosque

2007–2008

Architect: Moshe Safdie & Associates

Client: Nakheel Corporation

Image credits:

Michael McCann (124–125, 126, 127)

Crystal Computer Graphics Co., LTD (129 top)

John Horner (130, 131, 132–133)

Incheon International Airport Terminal 2

2011

Architect: Safdie Architects

Collaborators: Aum & Lee Architects & Associates, and Yooshin Architects & Engineers, Inc.

Client: Incheon International Airport Corporation

Image credits:

Neoscape Boston (134–135, 136, 140, 141, 143)

National Art Museum of China

2012

Architect: Safdie Architects

Collaborators: CCDI, Hao Sheng, Atelier Ten, ARUP, Lord Cultural Resources

Client: National Art Museum of China

Image credits:

Original sketch by Moshe Safdie (150–151)

Neoscape Boston (144–145, 147, 152, 153, 154–155, 156, 157)

Mogao Caves of Duhuang, Tokyo: Heibonsha, 1982 (146)

John Horner (148–149)

The Abrahamic Family House

2019

Architects: Safdie Architects

Collaborators: BuroHappold, Mott MacDonald, PWP Landscape Architecture; Pascal + Watson

Client: The Higher Committee for Human Fraternity

Image credits:

Original sketch by Moshe Safdie (161)

John Horner (170–171)

Neoscape Boston (158–159, 160, 162–163, 164–165, 166, 167, 168, 169)

The Lessons of Unbuilt Architecture

Original sketch by Moshe Safdie (172)

Credits & Acknowledgments

Original sketch by Moshe Safdie (178)

All other images courtesy of Safdie Architects

Acknowledgments

I thank the devoted members of my firm over the course of 50 years. I thank the brilliant engineers and other specialists I have had the good fortune to collaborate with, and last but not least, the committed clients who have made all this possible.

This publication would not have been possible without the thought-provoking questions of Michael Crosbie and the efforts of Christopher Mulvey, Michael Gericke, Matt McInerney, Tess Beckingham, and Robyn Payne.

I would also like to extend my gratitude to McGill University for their support in loaning materials from my Archive, which they have been the trusted custodians of for nearly 30 years.

—Moshe Safdie

About the Authors

Moshe Safdie, FAIA, is an architect, urban planner, educator, theorist, and author. Born In Haifa, Israel, in 1938, he graduated from McGill University in 1961 with a degree in architecture. After apprenticing with Louis Kahn, Safdie returned to Montreal to oversee the master plan for the 1967 World Exhibition. In 1964 he established his own firm to realize Habitat '67, an adaption of his undergraduate thesis. His firm has locations in Boston (its principal office), Toronto, Jerusalem, Singapore, and Shanghai. He has held teaching positions at Harvard, Yale, McGill, and Ben Gurion universities, and has lectured and been a visiting critic at dozens of others. In addition to numerous articles on the theory and practice of architecture, Safdie has written several books, such as *Habitat (1970), For Everyone a Garden* (1974), and *The City After the Automobile* (1997). Safdie has won dozens of international design awards, is a Companion of the Order of Canada, recipient of the Wolf Prize in Arts, winner of the Gold Medal of the Royal Architectural Institute of Canada, and received the Gold Medal of the American Institute of Architects.

Michael J. Crosbie, FAIA, is a writer, educator, and architect. He earned degrees in architecture from the Catholic University of America, where in 2015 he served as the Walton Visiting Critic. He has lectured at architecture schools in the USA and abroad. The author of, contributor to, and editor of more than 70 books on architecture and design, Crosbie has served as an editor of *Progressive Architecture* and *Architecture* magazines, and is the editor of the journal *Faith & Form*. He has authored hundreds of articles appearing in publications and digital media around the world. He is Professor of Architecture at the University of Hartford.